COMMERCE. DOT. COM

Concepts and skills

3rd edition

WORKBOOK

Elaine **Hamilton**

NELSON
CENGAGE Learning

Australia • Brazil • Japan • Korea • Mexico • Singapore • Spain • United Kingdom • United States

Commerce.dot.com Concepts and skills Workbook
3rd Edition
Elaine Hamilton
Robin Farr

Project editor: Robyn Beaver
Proofreader: Aynslie Harper
Text designer: Tim Harding
Cover designer: Luana Keays
Cover image: iStockphoto®
Permissions researchers: Wendy Duncan and Cara Gould
Production controller: Erin Dowling
Typeset by: Q2AMedia
Reprint: Alice Kane

Any URLs contained in this publication were checked for currency during the production process. Note, however, that the publisher cannot vouch for the ongoing currency of URLs.

© 2013 Cengage Learning Australia Pty Limited

For product information and technology assistance,
in Australia call **1300 790 853**;
in New Zealand call **0800 449 725**

For permission to use material from this text or product, please email **aust.permissions@cengage.com**

ISBN 978 0 17 025159 4

Cengage Learning Australia
Level 7, 80 Dorcas Street
South Melbourne, Victoria Australia 3205

Cengage Learning New Zealand
Unit 4B Rosedale Office Park
331 Rosedale Road, Albany, North Shore 0632, NZ

For learning solutions, visit **cengage.com.au**

Printed in Australia by Ligare Pty Limited.
2 3 4 5 6 7 8 22 21 20 19 18

Contents

Consumer choice

1.1 Commerce and choice

1. Choose two words from the following list to describe the shopper in this cartoon:

- Excited, confused, happy, interested, perplexed, angry, tired, upset.

....

- Why might he look like this?

....

- How do you feel when you go shopping?

....

- What things do you like the best about shopping?

....

- What things do you like the least?

....

- List the things that you know encourage you to buy when you go shopping.

....

2. Use the words, phrases and sentences from the list below to complete the following chart.

- a spending and saving plan
- an agreement (either written or spoken) between two parties; for example, a buyer and a seller.
- an intangible good that is provided by an individual or organisation.
- an item that is tangible. It can be seen or touched.
- collective wants
- consumer
- liability
- liquidity
- goods and services that we would like to consume
- needs
- selling the rights to use a business name, image or management system
- standard of living
- wants

....	Anyone who buys goods and services.
good	....
....	Goods essential to our survival.
....	Luxury or non-essential goods and services.
personal wants	....
....	Goods and services provided for the community by governments.
service	....
budget	....
....	A person's quality of life; a person's economic, social and personal wellbeing.
savings	....
contract	....
....	An individual's or business's financial responsibility for any losses.
....	Funds available for day-to-day spending.
franchise	....

ISBN 9780170251594

3. Put the following items into their correct category.

clothing	DVDs	food
schools	cars	movie tickets
perfume	police force	public transport
roads	shelter	water

Needs	Personal 'wants'	Collective 'wants'
....	....	....
....	....	....
....	....	....
....	....	....

4. Complete the following table to show the major points to be considered in decision making in these areas.

Employment: ....
....
....
....

Financial: ....
....
....
....
....
....

Business: ....
....
....
....

Legal: ....

Environmental: ....
....

1.2 Consumer decisions

1. Consider each item in the list below and then place it in its correct category.

bike, concert ticket, drinks, education, food, furniture, haircut, motor vehicle, newspaper, pen, takeaway food, television, train trip, washing machine, visit to doctor

Durable	Non-durable	Services
....	....	....
....	....	....
....	....	....
....	....	....
....	....	....

2. Complementary goods are those we purchase because two things 'go together'. List some complementary goods which we would purchase to go with each of the following.

Car ....

Computer ....

Television ....

3. a. Consumer decisions are sometimes made on the basis of brand. How many brand names are shown in the illustration above?

....

ISBN 9780170251594

b. Why do people buy products with a visible brand name? Give three reasons.

• ....

• ....

• ....

4. a. What is it called when you purchase an item on the spur of the moment without any planning?

....

b. Name two places where you are likely to indulge in this spur of the moment buying because the places are designed to encourage it.

• ....

• ....

c. List the six questions you should ask yourself before making a purchase to help you avoid spur of the moment buying.

i. ....

ii. ....

iii. ....

iv. ....

v. ....

vi. ....

5. a. Select the outlet that is at the top (most popular) of the shopping hierarchy and the one that is at the bottom (least popular).

planned centre   franchises
general (corner) store   independent speciality stores
supermarket   category killer

....

b. Why is shopping in the CBD is no longer as popular as it used to be? Give one reason.

....

c. Name the outlet that has most affected the popularity of corner stores.

....

6. a. Name two ways in which shopping can be done from home.

• ....

• ....

b. What are the two (2) main advantages of these?

• ....

• ....

7. The diagram below shows seven factors affecting your decision making as a consumer. Add the correct heading to the top of the correct box in the diagram.

Factors affecting consumer decisions

....
Can I obtain finance to help me make this purchase?

....
What is my budget?
Can I afford this good or service?

....
How is marketing used to lure me as a potential customer?

....
How do my age and gender influence my consumption habits?

....
What impact does the consumption of this product have on the environment?

....
What in-store service is available?
How easy is it to shop in this way?

....
Does this product have a warranty?
What after-sales service is available?

ISBN 9780170251594

1.3 Consumer protection

1. List eight areas in which you, as a consumer, have to be particularly wary of scams and rip-offs.

a. ....

b. ....

c. ....

d. ....

e. ....

f. ....

g. ....

h. ....

2. Rearrange into the correct order the following six steps in resolving a consumer complaint.

- Contact the state government's consumer affairs department
- Contact the business without delay
- Identify the problem
- Contact a court or tribunal
- Contact the relevant industry association or ombudsman
- Contact a mediation/conflict resolution service

a. ....

b. ....

c. ....

d. ....

e. ....

f. ....

3. Put these parts of a letter of complaint in the right order.

- a possible solution to the problem
- your name
- the date of the letter
- a clear description of the problem
- the receiver's name and address
- a statement of your rights

a. ....

b. ....

c. ....

d. ....

e. ....

f. ....

4. a. Complete the following sentence:

Any agreement to .... or .... and .... whether it is .... or spoken, is a form of ....

ISBN 9780170251594

b. Complete the table below, which outlines the six essential features of a contract:

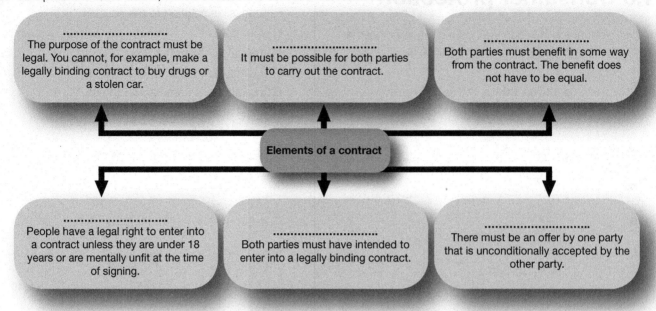

The purpose of the contract must be legal. You cannot, for example, make a legally binding contract to buy drugs or a stolen car.

It must be possible for both parties to carry out the contract.

Both parties must benefit in some way from the contract. The benefit does not have to be equal.

Elements of a contract

People have a legal right to enter into a contract unless they are under 18 years or are mentally unfit at the time of signing.

Both parties must have intended to enter into a legally binding contract.

There must be an offer by one party that is unconditionally accepted by the other party.

c. Consumers have **rights** which are protected by legislation and **responsibilities**. There are **organisations** which provide assistance in making sure consumers' rights are protected. Compile a table of these, using a summary of information on pages 25–27 of your textbook.

Rights (Consumer protection laws)	Responsibilities	Organisations providing assistance
		Government
		Independent

5. Match each phrase with its definition by drawing connecting lines.

a. consumer sovereignty   fit for the purpose for which a good is bought

b. merchantable quality   dishonest and unfair conduct by individuals or businesses providing goods and services to consumers

c. unconscionable conduct   the power of consumers to decide which business and products survive in the marketplace

ISBN 9780170251594

1.4 Payment choices

1. Your textbook lists nine methods of payment for goods and services. They are:

cash, direct debit, cheque, credit card, booking up, lay-by, Electronic Funds Transfer, BPay and EFTPOS.

Here is a list of clues that relate to these methods. Match them in the table below.

CLUE   **METHOD OF PAYMENT**

a. Makes it very easy to overspend!   ....

b. Excellent for negotiation of good prices!   ....

c. Plenty of time to pay with no interest charges!   ....

d. Use the phone or the Internet to transfer payment.   ....

e. Transfers money to pay as you purchase.   ....

f. Makes sure that bills are paid on time.   ....

g. Very secure but not accepted by everyone.   ....

h. Short-term credit method used in small communities.   ....

i. General term for all financial transactions carried out electronically ....

2. Complete the blank cheque using the information listed below it.

Date _____	The Bank of Australia	Date _____
To _____	Local Branch	
For _____	Pay _____ or bearer	
	The sum of _____	
	_____ $ [_____]	
Amount _____		
Balance _____	I.M. Wealthy	
1001038	1001038 082 117 16689 4444 _____	

- Today is 8th March 2014.
- You currently have $326.75 in your cheque account.
- You want to pay a bill for $250 to E.M. Services who have just repaired your air-conditioner.

- You want to make sure that the cheque is paid only to E.M. Services.
- Your name (for this exercise) is I.M. Wealthy.
- You want to note down how much you have left after you have paid this bill.

ISBN 9780170251594

3. The illustration relates to the article 'The Jetsons supermarket'.

a. Why does the author refer to the supermarket as 'The Jetsons Supermarket'?

....

....

....

b. Name the two items that Mrs Jetson needs in order to do her shopping in the supermarket.

• ....

• ....

c. What is the proper name of the microchip that would be on the label of every item in this futuristic supermarket?

....

d. Where are similar tags already being used?

....

e. Name three advantages of this system being used in factories and on farms.

....

....

Jake Nowakowski/Newspix

4. Name three transactions you can do using an ATM.

....

....

5. A few acronyms (words formed from the initial letters of other words) are listed below. Write down the words from which these acronyms are formed.

EFT   ....

EFTPOS   ....

ATM   ....

PIN   ....

ISBN 9780170251594

Personal finance

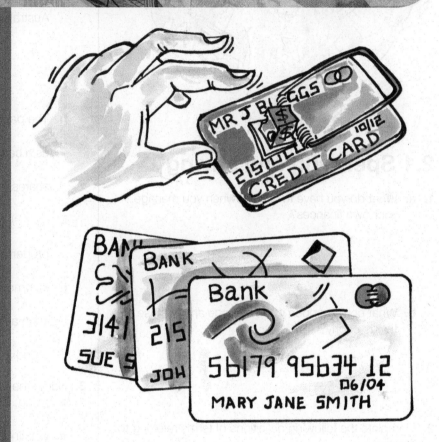

2.1 Spending and saving

1. a. What do you have to 'juggle' when you manage your own finances?

....

b. What could happen if you manage any of these things poorly?

....

2. Complete the following definitions of terms referring to income.

a. A .... is income received for work done based on the hours worked each week.

b. Income received each week for a job, usually irrespective of the number of .... worked, is called a ....

c. The income from providing a professional ...., such as legal advice or public speaking, is known as a ....

d. Commission is the income from acting as an ...., or go between, between .... and ....

e. The .... of .... over .... in running a business is called profit.

f. Payments made by the .... to ensure all Australians have a liveable income are called ....

g. .... is the income received from investments.

h. The payment made to a .... of a company as a cash reward for investing in that company's shares is called a ....

i. .... is the income received for the use of a property.

j. Income from the .... of a piece of work such as a song, a book or an invention is called a ....

3. Name the type of income that relates to each of the following. (There could be more than one answer.)

a. working for an employer

....

b. working and investing in various ways for yourself

....

c. the government

....

d. winning a competition

....

e. savings account

....

ISBN 9780170251594

4. Name the type of income related to each of the following terms.

a. overtime

....

b. agent

....

c. flexitime

....

d. self-employed

....

e. service

....

f. property

....

g. penalty rate

....

h. pension

....

i. shareholder

....

j. songs, books, inventions

....

5. Put the correct $ amounts into the spaces in the cartoon. Refer to page 39 of your text for help.

6. Our spending can be classified into .... and .... expenditure. Classify the following items as either fixed or variable by placing them in the correct column below.

clothes, insurance, computer software, food, fuel, furniture, DVD hire and/or purchase, electricity, books and magazines, rent, movie tickets, vehicle registration fees, shoes, house payments, Internet access, video games, gifts, phone charges

FIXED	VARIABLE
....	....
....	....
....	....
....	....
....	....
....	....
....	....
....	....
....	....

ISBN 9780170251594

7. Imagine your income is $300 per week. Think about how you would divide this amount among the seven spending and saving options in the cartoon. Write the amounts in the spaces beside each option. Discuss your decisions in small groups. (There is no right answer to this activity!)

2.2 Investing

1. Fill in the gaps in the following paragraph by using words from the list below.

   future needs, possess, wealth, money

   > We invest our .... in order to increase our
   >
   > .... (that is, the stock of things we
   >
   > ...., such as money, a house, works of art
   >
   > and shares) and provide for ....

2. The four main reasons people decide to invest are listed below. They are:

   - investing for extra income
   - investing for retirement
   - saving for a major purchase
   - saving for a 'rainy day'.

   Add the above in the correct places in the diagram opposite.

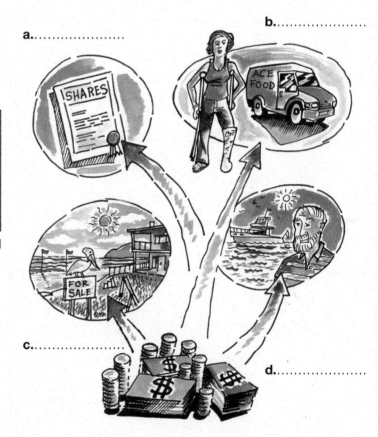

ISBN 9780170251594

3. An important point to remember in investing money is that the higher the return, the greater is the risk that we could lose our money.

Place the following in order of risk with the highest level of risk at the top of your list. NOTE: There could be more than one option on the same level.

term deposits

superannuation funds

passbook or savings account

investment account

government bonds and securities

share market

keycard accounts

managed funds

cash management accounts

property/real estate

....

....

....

....

....

....

4. Explain why banks can offer a higher rate of interest on long-term accounts than on accounts where your money is available on demand.

....

5. a. What does the abbreviation ASX stand for?

....

b. What are traded there?

....

c. What term is used to describe the share market when

- prices rise and returns are high

....

- prices fall and there are losses

....

d. What is bought and sold on the property market?

....

2.3 Borrowing

1. Fill in the gaps in the following box with these words:

bank, borrow, charges, cost, debt, existing, fixed, interest, legal, loan-establishment, principal, rates, repayments, spend, stamp duty, variable

People .... money because they wish to

.... more money than they have at the

moment. When you borrow money you are in

.... Debt causes difficulties if you have trouble

making the .... or you borrow more to

cover your .... debt. The money that is

borrowed is called the loan ....

You have to repay the principal and also the

.... Interest .... can be either

.... or .... Apart from interest

.............., lenders often add other charges to the

.... of a loan such as .... costs,

.... charges or .... fees.

Governments often charge ....

when a loan is taken out.

2. The illustration below shows only one institution – a savings bank – which lends money. Name five others.

a. ....

b. ....

c. ....

d. ....

e. ....

3. Which financial institution would be best to approach to get a loan for the following?
(Circle the correct answer/s.)

car   bank, building society, credit union, merchant bank, finance company, insurance company

house   bank, building society, credit union, merchant bank, finance company, insurance company

holiday   bank, building society, credit union, merchant bank, finance company, insurance company

credit for a large business   bank, building society, credit union, merchant bank, finance company, insurance company

finance for an industrial development   bank, building society, credit union, merchant bank, finance company, insurance company

4. Loan sharks such as Easy Loans may offer you a loan but what four important issues should you consider before you accept such a loan?

• ....

• ....

• ....

• ....

5. The most important thing to consider when choosing a credit card is

a. whether or not there is an annual fee to pay.

b. how long an interest-free period it allows.

c. the interest rate charged.

d. all of the above.

ISBN 9780170251594

6. Circle the three <u>correct</u> words in the following sentence :

Credit cards may encourage people to <u>spend/save</u> <u>less/more</u> than they can <u>earn/afford</u>.

7. List the seven factors/items that financial institutions take into consideration in deciding whether or not to give you a loan.

- ....
- ....
- ....
- ....
- ....
- ....
- ....

8. Fill in the missing words on the labels below.

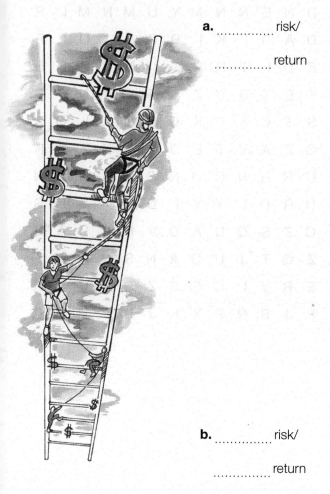

a. .... risk/
.... return

b. .... risk/
.... return

2.4 Managing your finances

1. Before deciding whether to save, spend, invest or borrow, you need to consider whether or not you are fully informed about various financial institutions and what they offer. List four sources of this financial advice.

....

....

....

....

2. Name three laws or organisations which are designed to help protect your rights in financial dealings.

....

....

....

PREMIUMS   CLAIM PAYOUTS

3. a. What name is given to the money, paid regularly, to an insurance company to protect you against loss/damage?

....

b. The illustration above shows three examples where people will need to claim insurance. What are they?

....

....

....

ISBN 9780170251594

c. What is the other main classification of insurance that includes life, income and health insurance?

....

4. a. Give the name of the planning tool that you can create and which enables you to work out:
- how much you have in income
- how much you spend
- how much you can save or need to save.

....

b. Give the correct name for the shortfall if your spending is greater than your income.

....

5. a. If up have run up a lot of debt because of poor financial management, who are the first people to turn to for advice? Why?

....

....

....

b. If this doesn't work, what can you do next?

....
....
....
....
....

6. Use the words below to complete the wonderword. The words can run vertically, horizontally, diagonally and backwards.

savings	financial	services
ACCC	banks	investing
bankruptcy	loans	spending
interest rates	budgeting	risk
credit rating	credit cards	return
income	debt collector	advice
industry	borrowing	

```
D I X U C Y B O R R O W I N G
E N F Z R G A A N R U T E R N
B T D N E N N M Y U M N M L P
T E D A D I K I R R R J O I F
C R E D I T R A T I N G C I E
O E K E T S U Z S E L X N J R
L S S T C E P K U G G A I Q Z
L T G Z A V T E D I N D Z X F
E R U H R N C H N C S I U F N
C A U R D I Y Y I D C T V B S
T T C Z S Q U A D V I C E A K
O E Z O T J L O A N S N A N S
R S E R V I C E S Z D K G K R
D F F J B N F X K J U L P S Q
```

ISBN 9780170251594

Law and society

3.1 The legal framework

1. a. List three things that laws are designed to do.

- to ....

- to ....

- to ....

b. What kind of situation would there be if there were no laws?

....

....

c. Name two very familiar places that have their own rules and regulations.

....

....

d. Describe how rules and regulations differ from laws.

....

....

2. a. Add the following labels to the correct boxes in the diagram below so that it correctly shows the court hierarchy in Australia.

- Federal Court
- High Court
- Family Court
- State District Courts
- State Local Courts
- State Supreme Courts

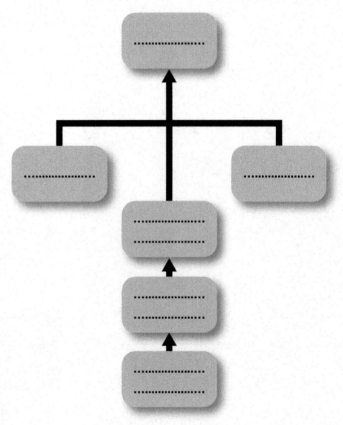

b. Which three of these are NSW courts?

- ....

- ....

- ....

ISBN 9780170251594

c. **i.** Give another name for the Local Court.

....

ii. Name two types of offences this court deals with. Explain briefly what they are.

- ....

- ....

d. **i.** Who presides over a District Court?

....

ii. Name two matters a District Court deals with.

- ....

- ....

iii. Which of these requires a jury?

....

iv. How many people are on a jury?

....

e. The Supreme Court in a state hears the most difficult cases and those that involve difficult points of law – but what else can it do that other courts can't?

....

3. **a.** Name five matters that are dealt with by Federal courts.

- ....

- ....

- ....

- ....

- ....

b. Outline the two main functions of the High Court of Australia.

- ....

- ....

4. The illustration below shows a typical courtroom. Label the following people in the courtroom correctly.

- Court reporter
- Defence lawyer
- Defendant
- Judge
- Judge's assistant
- Jury
- Prosecutor
- Public gallery
- Witness

5. a. Complete the following table.

Court	Presiding officer	Method of address
• Local	....	....
• District, Supreme	....	....
• High and Family	....	....

b. Are the following people 'for', 'against' or 'neutral' with regards to an accused person during a trial?

- Prosecutor ....
- Defence lawyer ....
- Jury ....

3.2 Areas of law

1. Use the information on pages 65–69 of your textbook to compile a summary table of how laws may be classified. Some boxes have been done for you. (Hint: Look for sub-headings in the text.)

General Classification	Subdivisions	Purpose
a. PUBLIC	i. Criminal	to protect the general public from harm
✕		
OR CIVIL		
✕	ii. Property	
✕		to help people receive compensation if they have been inconvenienced by the actions of other people

2. Compile another table showing the six main types of criminal activity with examples of some types of these crimes. The first one is done for you.

a.	Crimes against persons	homicide, manslaughter, assault
b.		
c.		
d.		
e.		
f.		

ISBN 9780170251594

b. Which court deals with family matters?

....

5. Complete the following passage using the words below.

codification, common, English, Federal, High Court, judges, precedent, statute

Common law is unique to those legal systems that

adopt .... Common Law. Common Laws

are based on the rules of .... and lower

courts must follow the decisions. This is known as

following ....

In Australia, the Supreme Courts of each state,

the .... of Australia and the ....

Court are all supreme courts and are the only courts

that have the power to set precedents and make

.... law. To ensure important common

laws are not lost, parliamentarians often act to make

common law into .... law. This process is

known as ....

3. a. Write some notes on the impression the above cartoon gives you about the United States.

....

....

....

b. Write two sentences on whether you think this picture could be applied to Australia.

....

....

....

4. a. Name four areas that are regulated by family law.

- ....

- ....

- ....

- ....

6. a. What values in society influence our laws?

....

b. Because these influences can change, laws must be changeable.

i. Who can change:

- statute law? ....

- common law? ....

- the constitution? ....

ii. Which takes precedence if there is a conflict, statute or common law?

....

ISBN 9780170251594

7. Statute law is the most common form of law-making in Australia. These laws are made by parliaments and the procedure is shown in the flow-chart below. Seven important pieces of information have been left out of the diagram. They are:

- ....
- ....
- ....

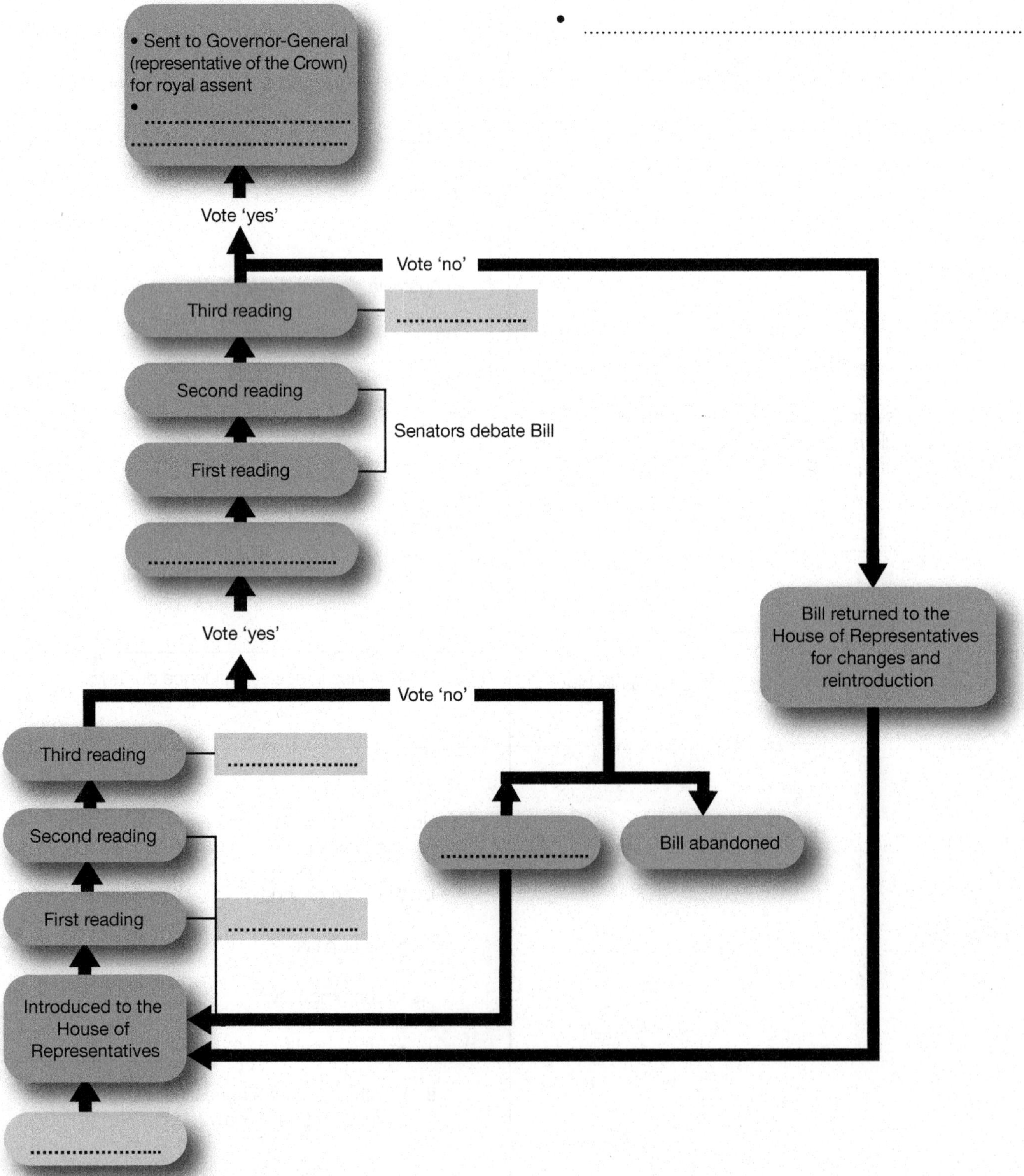

- ....
- ....
- ....

- ....

• Sent to Governor-General (representative of the Crown) for royal assent

- ....

Vote 'yes'

Vote 'no'

Third reading — ....

Second reading

First reading — Senators debate Bill

....

Vote 'yes'

Vote 'no'

Bill returned to the House of Representatives for changes and reintroduction

Third reading — ....

Second reading

First reading — ....

....   Bill abandoned

Introduced to the House of Representatives

....

ISBN 9780170251594

8. Write a paragraph commenting on the following:

The worst thing about shoplifting is getting caught.

....

....

....

....

....

3.3 Using the legal system

1. Fill in the gaps in the passage below by using the following words in the correct place.

1972	access	barristers
complex	courts	day
difficult	disputes	fair
fair trial	freedom	lawyer
legal	Legal Aid	ourselves
processes	resolve	terminology

The .... system exists to help all Australians

resolve .... in a peaceful and fair way. However,

we do not have an automatic right to a .... We can

represent .... in the court but this is often

.... as the law is .... and most people

struggle to understand the legal .... and

.... associated with the operation of our courts.

    While there is no automatic right to a lawyer,

there is a right to a .... However, ...

(lawyers who are trained to represent clients in ....)

often charge several thousand dollars for each ....

they represent their client in court which means that

many people are unable to afford .... to the court

system and use it to .... their disputes. In criminal

matters, when a person's .... is at stake, this

creates an even more serious problem. To ensure that

people obtain .... treatment from the legal system,

.... was introduced by the Whitlam Labor

Government in ....

2. a. Name the organisation that provides legal assistance to people who are unable to afford their own lawyer.

....

b. How much time is available free from this organisation for all people?

....

c. What three tests must people pass in order to get further free legal assistance?

- ....
- ....
- ....

d. Which group of people are not subject to two of these tests?

....

3. Suggest three reasons why the person in this illustration may not know her rights.

- ....
- ....
- ....

ISBN 9780170251594

4. a. Complete the diagram below by adding four factors that affect access to the legal system.

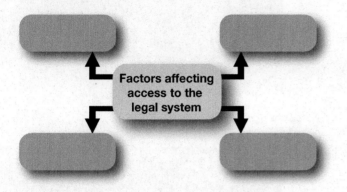

b. Why is cost a problem for people involved in civil law matters?

....

c. Name three bodies/Acts that have been established to help overcome this problem.

- ....

- ....

- ....

d. Name another area of law for which Legal Aid does not provide assistance.

....

e. What method has been introduced to try to resolve these cases without going to court?

....

f. Describe why time is a factor affecting access to the legal system.

....

....

....

....

g. Name two aspects of a court hearing that are very formal and which can be confusing and daunting to many people.

- ....

- ....

h. Name two other factors – not shown in the diagram – that reduce access to the legal system for many people.

- ....

- ....

ISBN 9780170251594

4

Employment issues

4.1 The workplace

1. a. Name each job represented in the illustration above. Indicate whether each job is a trade or profession and what level of education each job requires.

....
....
....
....
....

b. Which job(s) pictured appeal to you the most?

....

2. Match the following terms with their correct definitions.

employee   full-time employment
blue-collar worker   unemployed
part-time employment   white-collar worker
self-employed   casual employment

- being without a job but able and willing to work

....

- a person working under the control or direction of another in return for a wage or salary.

....

- people who operate their own business

....

- a manual labourer

....

- a regular job with benefits, which include paid annual leave

....

- temporary work

....

- someone in a professional, administrative, technical or clerical position

....

- working fewer than 35 hours per week

....

3. a. Discuss why it is now expected that people will change jobs/careers four or five times in their working life.

....

b. Name five other factors that have changed the labour force significantly over the past few decades.

- ....

- ....

- ....

- ....

- ....

ISBN 9780170251594

4. a. Give the general name for tertiary, quarternary and quinary industries.

....

b. Name the industry sector – primary, secondary or services – which has grown significantly since 1966.

....

c. Which sector has declined most?

....

d. Name four activities in the sector named in (c.) above.

....

5. There has been a great increase in the number of part-time workers since 1990. In which industries is this trend greatest?

....

6. Education and training for employment provide a range of personal and social benefits. List at least three of each.

- personal

....
....
....

- social (beneficial to society)

....
....
....

7. a. Name four conditions of employment that should be detailed in a **contract of employment**.

- ....

- ....

- ....

- ....

b. There are two types of employment contracts – formal and informal. Write 'formal' or 'informal' underneath each of the following terms to indicate which kind of employment contract the term is associated with.

- Enterprise bargaining

....

- Not easily enforced

....

- Verbal

....

- Fair Work Australia

....

- Enterprise agreement

....

8. a. List four reasons why you may be unemployed.

- ....

- ....

- ....

- ....

b. Name the year of highest unemployment in Australia and give the unemployment rate of that year.

....
....

c. Identify at least three problems that can be associated with long-term unemployment.

....
....
....
....

ISBN 9780170251594

4.2 Employment relations

1. List at least five factors that help to make a good working environment.

....

....

....

....

....

....

2. Many conditions of the workplace are governed by legislation. Which laws govern:

a. safe working conditions?

- ....

- ....

b. discrimination?

- ....

- ....

- ....

- ....

- ....

- ....

3. If you are asked to leave your job, you may want to check whether your dismissal has been <u>unlawful</u> or <u>unfair</u>.

a. Define unlawful dismissal.

....

....

b. Give an example of unlawful dismissal which relates to trade unions.

....

....

c. To whom and when do you apply/complain about unlawful dismissal?

....

....

....

d. Define unfair dismissal.

....

....

e. To whom and when do you apply/complain about unfair dismissal?

....

....

4. a. Name two terms used to describe the situation when an employee has to leave their job because their work is no longer required by their employer due to economic, technological or other reasons.

- ....

- ....

b. Identify the benefits an employee can receive in these circumstances.

....

....

....

....

c. Who is generally better off – an employee who accepts voluntary redundancy or one or accepts involuntary redundancy?

....

5. a. Who makes the policy for an employee's privacy?

....

b. Are employers allowed to listen to or record telephone calls made by employees?

....

....

....

c. Name another area of communication where there is an issue of privacy that is not clearly defined.

....

d. Are employers generally allowed to look at emails? Why?

....

....

7. List three disadvantages for the worker of outsourcing and piecework.

....

....

....

8. a. Describe the most likely situation that will lead to an industrial dispute.

....

....

b. List five ways in which disputes can be resolved.

- ....

- ....

- ....

- ....

- ....

6. Complete the table to show some of the roles of trade unions and employer associations.

TRADE UNIONS	EMPLOYER ASSOCIATIONS

ISBN 9780170251594

9. In your own words fill in the Steps (1–4) in the industrial dispute depicted in the cartoon below.

....
....
....
....
....
....
....
....
....
....
....
....
....
....
....
....
....

4.3 Taxation and superannuation

1. Use the words below to complete the following table.

Capital gains tax, GST, Payroll tax, Income tax, Fringe benefits tax, Stamp duty, Rates, Excise duty

Table 4.3a Overview of the different types of taxes in Australia

Tax	Description	Liability to pay
	A federal government tax levied on salary and wages	Payable by the person or company who earns the income
	A tax on goods and services (currently 10 per cent of the price of the good or service)	Payable by businesses but passed on to consumers and included in the prices we pay
	A tax applied on the production of certain goods, such as cigarettes, alcohol and petrol	Payable by businesses but passed on to consumers and included in the prices we pay
	A state tax on businesses with a wages bill over $689 000	Payable by businesses at a rate of approximately 6 per cent of the total wages bill
	A state tax on certain transactions, such as the sale of a house or car	Payable by the purchaser of the asset
	A local government tax on the value of a property	Payable by the owner of the property
	A federal government tax on the money someone receives when they sell an asset that they purchased after 19 September 1985	Payable by the seller of the asset
	A federal government tax on fringe benefits paid to an employee	Payable by the employer

2. Fill in the gaps in the following passage by using these words in their correct places.

compulsory, deductions, employers, financial, governments, group certificate, income, income tax, PAYE, public, social security, tax return, wages, welfare

Taxes are .... payments made to

.... by individuals, businesses and

other groups and provide governments with their main

source of .... This money is then spent on

.... goods and services with the largest area

of spending being on .... and

.... The largest source of government

income comes from .... which is taken

out of people's .... or salary by their

.... before they receive it. This is known as

the pay as you earn (....................) system.

At the end of the .... year, each employee

receives a .... showing income earned

and tax paid. Employees then send the group

certificate with a .... which shows their

income and .... to the ATO, which then

notifies them if they have paid too much or too little

income tax for the year.

3. As income increases, the tax rate increases. The tax rates for 2011–12 are shown in the table below. Using these figures, calculate the tax payable by people with the following taxable incomes:

a. $5000 ....

b. $6001 ....

c. $55 000 ....

d. $80 000 ....

e. $200 000 ....

Tax rates for 2011–12

Taxable income	Tax on this income*
$0–$6000	Nil
$6001–$37 000	15 cents for each $1 over $6000
$37 001–$80 000	$4650 plus 30 cents for each $1 over $37 000
$80 001–$180 000	$17 550 plus 37 cents for each $1 over $80 000
$180 001 and over	$54 550 plus 45 cents for each $1 over $180 000

*The above rates *do not* include the Medicare levy of 1.5 per cent of an employee's taxable income.

ISBN 9780170251594

4. Use the example of Mr Harvey's financial situation shown in the tables on pages 113 and 114 to answer the following questions.

a. What was Mr Harvey's total income?

....

b. What were his total deductions?

....

c. What was his taxable income?

....

d. How much tax had he paid during the year?

....

e. How much tax should he have paid, including the Medicare Levy?

....

f. Was he due for a refund or did he have to pay?

....

g. How much?

....

5. a. Give a reason for contributing to superannuation.

....

b. Where does most of your superannuation come from?

....

c. Name the current rate (percentage) paid into superannuation. What percentage will it eventually rise to?

....

d. Explain what a personal contribution to superannuation is.

....

e. Name the time when a person can collect their superannuation.

....

6. Find the following words in the wonderword below. The words can run vertically, horizontally, diagonally and backwards.

trade unions	ACTU	enterprise
business	group	awards
strike	wages	meeting
laws	working	conditions
go-slow	pay	scabs
sit-down	bans	agreement
contract	picket line	negotiation
AIRC		

```
W  C  S  S  E  N  I  S  U  B
W  O  R  K  I  N  G  I  T  A
G  N  I  T  E  E  M  T  E  N
O  D  S  C  A  B  S  -  S  S
P  I  N  A  W  A  R  D  S  T
I  T  E  G  R  A  D  O  L  R
C  I  G  R  O  U  P  W  A  A
K  O  O  E  K  C  I  N  W  D
E  N  T  E  R  P  R  I  S  E
T  S  I  M  A  C  T  U  K  U
L  Y  A  E  P  E  S  I  S  N
I  A  T  N  A  I  R  C  E  I
N  P  I  T  L  T  P  U  G  O
E  G  O  -  S  L  O  W  A  N
C  O  N  T  R  A  C  T  W  S
```

Use the remaining uncircled letters to fill in two missing words below.

.... often occur in the workplace. They are, however, usually resolved through negotiation between employees and employers and with the help of trade unions and employer associations.

ISBN 9780170251594

5

Investing

5.1 Investing: an overview

1. Match the following words with their definitions.

income   negative gearing

investment   mortgage

ethical investing   collateral

unit trust   capital gain

capital loss   equity

- occurs when the sale price for an asset is greater than the initial cost

....

- an asset promised to a lender in case the borrower is unable to meet the loan repayments

....

- investing in assets that are considered to be morally sound

....

- regular payments from an investment

....

- an asset purchased with the intention of producing a capital gain or income, or both

....

- a loan used to fund the purchase of a property

....

- an investment where the interest on the borrowing exceeds the income from the investment

....

- a pooled investment or managed fund

....

- occurs when the sale price for an asset is less than the initial cost

....

- the value of an investment less the amount of money owing on the investment

....

2. a. Explain the difference between 'saving' and 'investing'.

....

....

....

b. Name three long-term goals of investing.

- ....

- ....

- ....

3. a. Money can be received on an investment while it is owned; or money can be made when an investment is sold at a profit. One of these is called 'income' and the other 'capital gain'. Which is which?

....

....

ISBN 9780170251594

b. Give the term to describe the situation when an investment is sold for less than it cost.

....

4. a. Define an investment portfolio. How much money do you need to begin one?

....

....

....

b. Explain the difference between a mortgage and any other loan.

....

....

....

c. What term is used to refer to a mortgaged property?

....

5. a. Explain briefly why some people are happy if the income gained from their investment is less than their repayments.

....

....

b. List three or more disadvantages or risks that can be associated with this.

- ....
- ....
- ....
- ....
- ....

c. Define equity loan.

....

....

....

6. a. Explain ethical investing.

....

....

....

b. Another name for it is:

....

....

c. Define negative screening.

....

....

d. Define positive screening.

....

....

ISBN 9780170251594

5.2 Investment options

1. List the four major investment options.

- ....
- ....
- ....
- ....

2. a. Link each of the above with one of the terms in the list below.

   i. real estate   ....

   ii. dividend   ....

   iii. term deposit   ....

   iv. bonds   ....

b. Explain the basic difference between a bond and a term deposit.

....

d. Why do investors often favour property over other forms of investment? Give one reason.

....

e. Name the items bought and sold in the building pictured below.

....

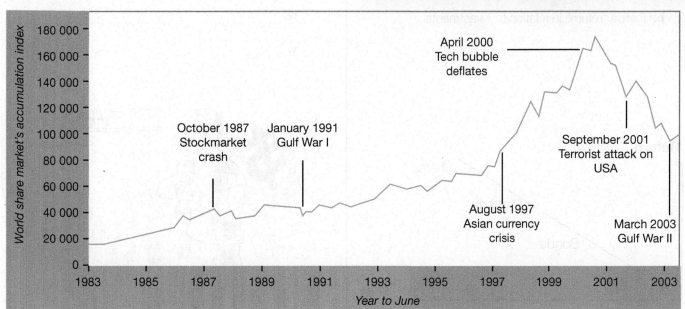

c. Choose the statement from the list below which best explains the graph above.

   i. Share prices rise after a world crisis.

   ii. World share prices have increased overall since 1983.

   iii. The price of shares is continuously rising.

   iv. Share prices drop every five years.

3. a. Identify four things that are typically purchased in a fund management account.

....

ISBN 9780170251594

b. Define pooled funds.

....

c. Identify the advantage of pooled funds.

....

d. Name four other advantages of investing in managed funds.

- ....

- ....

- ....

- ....

4. a. Define 'risk' in relation to investments.

....

b. Define "return" in relation to investments.

....

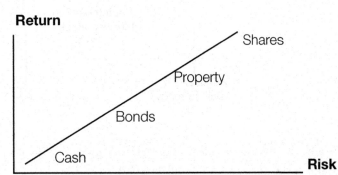

Return

Shares

Property

Bonds

Cash

Risk

c. According to the diagram above:

i. which investment has the lowest risk?

....

ii. which investment gives the highest return?

....

iii. which has the higher risk – bonds or property?

....

iv. which has the lower return – bonds or property?

....

5. a. Give the name for investing in a variety of investment types and in various investments within each type.

....

b. Name one advantage of this.

....

6. a. Name the different kinds of investments shown in the cartoon below.

i. ....

ii. ....

iii. ....

iv. ....

v. ....

ISBN 9780170251594

b. Complete this table with regard to the advantages and disadvantages of the different types of investment listed.

Type of investment	Disadvantages	Advantages
property		
cash and fixed interest		
shares		

5.3 Investment planning

1. List three factors to be taken into consideration before establishing an investment portfolio.

- ....
- ....
- ....

2. a. Create a record sheet that could be used to maintain essential records of investments.

Name of investment	Date acquired	Purchase cost	Sale				Financial returns		
			% sold	% still held	Date of sale	Income from sale	Amount received	Date received	Total returns

....

- ....
- ....
- ....
- ....

b. Name one way of measuring the performance of investments.

....

....

3. a. List some situations that would suggest an investor's portfolio may need to be adjusted.

- ....

  ....

- ....

  ....

- ....

b. Name two key issues which can affect the current investment environment.

- ....

- ....

4. a. Name the legislation relating to investment which was passed in NSW in 2000.

....

b. Identify the change that has resulted from that legislation.

....

....

c. Describe how this is done.

....

....

....

....

d. Explain what is meant by 'comparison rate'.

....

....

....

e. Identify the group these new rules apply to.

....

....

....

f. Describe two features of the loans that these new rules apply to.

- ....

  ....

  ....

- ....

  ....

ISBN 9780170251594

5. Complete the crossword below.

Across

1 An investor's share of a company's profit

3 Regular payments from an investment

9 The term used to describe the true rate of interest. It includes both the interest rate and any fees and charges (two words)

11 An asset purchased with the intention of producing a capital gain or income, or both, for the owner

12 Borrowing for the purpose of investment, such as purchasing a share portfolio or using a mortgage to purchase a house

14 The amount of money received from an investment each year. It may consist of income and/or capital growth and is usually expressed as a percentage

Down

2 Spreading investments over a range of asset sectors with the aim of reducing risk

4 Occurs when the sale price for an asset is greater than the initial cost (two words)

5 Occurs when the sale price for an asset is less than the initial cost (two words)

6 Money invested for a fixed period of time. Interest is paid at regular intervals (two words)

7 An asset promised to a lender in case the borrower is unable to meet the loan repayments

8 A loan used to fund the purchase of a property

10 A loan where the equity in an asset is used as collateral for the loan that is taken out to buy further assets (two words)

13 The level of uncertainty associated with a particular investment

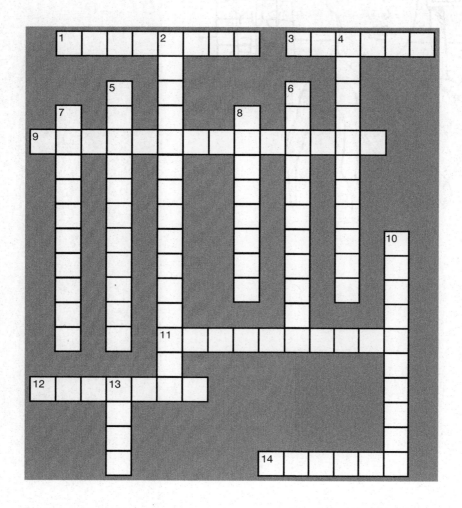

ISBN 9780170251594

6

Promoting and selling

6.1 The selling process

1. Brainstorm and note down all the ways people are encouraged to buy things in our society.

....
....
....
....

2. a. Name the two major factors in the selling process of a good or service.

....
....
....

b. The sale of a product generally requires choice on the part of the buyer/consumer. List the five factors that will influence a consumer in his/her choice.

- ....
- ....
- ....
- ....
- ....

c. If you were choosing to buy the following products, which factor would/should you place first in importance in your decision?

- ice cream ....
- weed killer ....
- a car ....
- a fur coat ....
- food ....

(You may have other correct answers; discuss with your teacher.)

3. Advertising is a major promotion strategy. List 10 places where we frequently are exposed to advertising.

....
....
....

4. a. Logos are a form of advertising. Draw five logos that you are familiar with.

ISBN 9780170251594

b. Some brand names become so well known that they are eventually used as the generic name for the product. For example, the British quite often refer to vacuuming as 'hoovering'. Name four other examples of this.

....
....
....
....

5. Outline the difference between product endorsement and sponsorship.

....
....
....
....

6. The name of the stadium pictured below changed from Stadium Australia to Telstra Stadium and now to ANZ Stadium. How and why did this happen?

....
....

Getty Images

7. a. Give the correct term for deliberately displaying a product in a movie for payment.

....

b. List five recognisable products that James Bond uses in the movie *Die Another Day*.

....
....
....
....
....

8. a. Match 'guerrilla marketing', 'direct marketing' and 'junk mail' with the terms below.

- phone, mail and email   ....

- stunts   ....

- advertising flyers   ....

9. a. Give the general name for the following selling/advertising methods: specials/discounts/prize offers/free samples/coupons/interest-free offers

....

b. Name two other examples.

- ....

- ....

10.a. Define upselling.

....

b. Give two examples.

....
....

11. Name two major industries that use free publicity of new products to supplement their paid advertising.

....

ISBN 9780170251594

12.a. Define stereotype.

....

....

b. Name one major factor used in stereotyping.

....

c. Explain the problem with this.

....

....

13. Explain what is meant by sexual exploitation in advertising.

....

....

6.2 Targeting consumers

1. Write down what this cartoon is suggesting about advertising.

....

....

....

2. Match the following terms with their definitions below.

bait and switch advertising; focus group; market research; mass marketing; niche marketing; sale price manipulation; self-regulation; target market

- Ethical standards and complaint resolution procedures put in place and maintained by an industry group.

....

- A specific demographic or social group to which an advertiser wishes to appeal.

....

- Marking goods with a sale price that is higher than the regular price.

....

- A group of potential customers who give their opinions about a campaign developed to promote a particular good or service.

....

- Advertising a product for sale when there is little or no stock of the product available.

....

- Promotional campaigns targeting quite small groups of potential customers.

....

- Promotional campaigns targeting a large proportion of the population.

....

- The gathering of information about the needs and desires of potential customers.

....

3. Name the target markets for the following items and when/where they are most likely to be advertised.

music CDs
- ....
- ....

car tools
- ....
- ....

anti-wrinkle cream • ....

• ....

toys • ....

• ....

4. a. Give the name of the approach used to advertise a product used by a large part of the population.

....

b. Name a product suitable for this kind of marketing.

....

5. If a product is aimed at a relatively small or exclusive market where cost of the product may not be an issue, what type of marketing is generally used?

....

6. a. Explain how a manufacturer identifies a target market.

....

b. Explain how surveys are generally conducted.

....

7. a. Because of legal or ethical issues not all products can be advertised. Give one well-known example of a product that cannot be advertised.

....

b. Name two organisations that check on the amounts and kinds of advertising shown.

• ....

• ....

c. Give the correct term for this checking.

....

8. a. Name three unethical promotional strategies.

....

....

b. Name two groups that can give advice and help to people who get into financial problems through overspending.

• ....

• ....

6.3 Applying selling techniques

1. Apart from promotional strategies, name some other factors used to help sales in the marketplace.

• ....

• ....

• ....

• ....

2. Explain why companies monitor sales of their products before, during and after their advertising campaigns.

....

3. In what two ways can a company gather information about brand recognition and the effectiveness of different selling techniques?

....

ISBN 9780170251594

6.4 Current issues in promoting and selling products

1. What issue is being suggested by the cartoon above?

   ....

   ....

2. Name four methods of product promotion that can sometimes intrude on our privacy.

   • ....

   • ....

   • ....

   • ....

3. Explain the change that has happened with the introduction of new technologies in terms of the interaction between buyer and seller.

   ....

4. List two important things to remember as a cautious buyer.

   a. ....

   ....

   b. ....

   ....

5. Define
   a. hidden advertising
   b. spam

   a. ....

   ....

ISBN 9780170251594

b. ....

....

....

....

6. a. The advertising of alcohol and tobacco products is highly regulated. Explain why.

....

....

....

....

....

b. Those who argue against the restriction of promoting alcohol and tobacco products claim that there is no real evidence that promotion of these products influences consumption and that it is the product, not the advertising, that should be regulated.

Think about this and then comment on it.

....

....

....

....

7. The following table lists the factors that differentiate similar products. The explanations in the second column are not in the correct order. Match them with the correct factor.

Factor	Explanation
service	whether the product reflects the values of a particular group
convenience	whether the product is recyclable and whether minimal resources were used to produce it
value	whether the product is easy to obtain
social factors	whether the product is economical and well worth the price paid for it
environmental factors	whether the product works well

a. service

....

....

b. convenience

....

....

c. value

....

....

d. social factors

....

....

e. environmental factors

....

....

ISBN 9780170251594

8. Complete the crossword below.

Across

2 The gathering of information about the needs and desires of potential consumers (two words)

3 Promoting a good or service in order to increase sales and profits or to inform the public

4 Promotional campaigns targeting quite small groups of potential customers (two words)

7 Ethical standards and complaint resolution procedures put in place and maintained by an industry group (two words, hyphenated)

8 Promotion of goods and services via the telephone

9 Promotional campaigns targeting a large proportion of the population (two words)

10 A type of marketing that is flexible and unconventional

11 Advertising flyers delivered via the letterbox (two words)

Down

1 The prominent display of products in movies and television programs (two words)

5 A specific demographic or social group that an advertiser wishes to appeal to (two words)

6 Personally addressed, businesslike letters containing advertising material (two words)

7 Brand strengthening via the funding of elite sporting personalities and teams

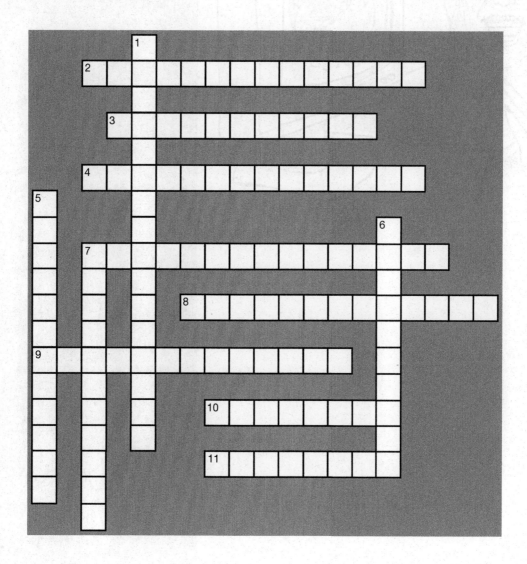

7

E-commerce

7.1 The scope of e-commerce

1. a. Define e-commerce.

....

....

....

b. What is ICT an abbreviation for?

....

c. Name four countries that make greater use of ICT than Australia.

....

d. Name two everyday examples of e-commerce.

....

2. a. What does the cartoon at the top right of this page suggest to you about shopping?

....

b. What is the primary means of carrying out e-commerce transactions?

....

c. Name three other uses of the Internet.

- ....

- ....

- ....

3. a. The three main users of e-commerce are businesses, consumers and government departments. The following abbreviations show the connection between these. Match them correctly.

B2B, B2C, C2C, G2C

E-commerce between

- consumers   ....

- businesses   ....

- a business and
  a consumer   ....

- government and
  a consumer   ....

ISBN 9780170251594

b. What, then, do the initials B, C and G stand for in those abbreviations?

- ....
- ....
- ....

c. What does the number '2' stand for?

....

4. a. Name three advantages that e-commerce has over the more traditional ways of transacting business.

- ....
- ....
- ....

b. Why are business costs generally lower with e-commerce?

....

5. Match the following words with their definitions.

spam, real time, banner, backup, modem, online, downloading

Connected to the Internet.

....

Loading information from one computer onto another.

....

A copy of a computer file, directory or disk make for safekeeping.

....

A narrow strip across the top of a webpage that carries a logo, the website's name or advertising.

....

A device used to connect two computers via a telephone line.

....

Events that occur on the Internet at the same time as they occur in real life.

....

Emails that have not been requested by the receiver.

....

7.2 The e-commerce user

1. List six ways in which a consumer can make use of e-commerce.

- ....
- ....
- ....
- ....
- ....
- ....

ISBN 9780170251594

2. Compile a table showing at least five advantages and five disadvantages of online shopping.

Advantages	Disadvantages

3. a. Which of the disadvantages of online shopping has largely been overcome by the use of SSL technology?

....

b. What do the letters SSL stand for in SSL technology?

....

c. What is the name given to the system of hiding information by using a code?

....

d. There are two places on a website where you can check whether your payments are secure. List them:

- ....

- ....

e. Name the three Australian laws that have been introduced specifically to deal with the new technology in the following ways:

- to outlaw activities such as hacking, spreading viruses, etc.

....

- to make paper and electronic transactions equal in law

....

- to make the Privacy Act 1998 apply to the private as well as the public sector

....

4. Refer to the shopping checklist below. Tick the boxes that are relevant for the purchase of (i) an item to be purchased from an Australian business and (ii) an item to be purchased from overseas.

From Australia	From overseas	
☐	☐	compared prices and 'shopped around'
☐	☐	ensured the business provides its contact name and address
☐	☐	verified the authenticity of an Australian business by checking the online ABN directory (all Australian businesses must have an Australian business number, or ABN)
☐	☐	telephoned or emailed the business to obtain details of its product (when dealing with a business for the first time)
☐	☐	obtained the exact details on the following:

- delivery or freight charges
- goods and services tax (GST)
- method of delivery
- exchange rates*
- import duties*

(*Important when dealing with overseas businesses.)

From Australia	From overseas	
☐	☐	found out whether it is legal to import certain goods or services from overseas into Australia
☐	☐	made sure the website is SSL secure
☐	☐	printed out my order (that is, made a hard copy) for my own records and double-checked all the details

5. a. Apart from speed and convenience, what is the other great advantage of online banking?

....

b. Name four examples of this:

- ....
- ....

- ....
- ....

c. Name three ways in which banks make funds transfer safe.

- ....
- ....
- ....

6. Name two organisations you can go to for advice on e-commerce issues.

- ....
- ....

7. There are some legitimate means and some scams used on the Internet to attract our attention as consumers. Which of the two categories do each of the following belong to?

- Pyramid scheme

....

- Use of a button to take you to a company's website

....

- Use of a purchased keyword

....

- Opportunity to view 'adult' images in return for credit card details

....

- Opportunity to get free access to adult material by downloading a 'viewer' computer program

....

- Use of banners

....

ISBN 9780170251594

7.3 Current issues in e-commerce

1. Why is it important that we, as e-commerce consumers, keep up to date with the technology revolution?

....

....

....

2. What, in general, are the three major steps you can take to protect yourself in your e-commerce transactions?

- ....
- ....
- ....

3. a. In a sentence, state what 'e-law' is.

....

....

4. a. What particular area of law relating to intellectual property is gaining a lot of attention because it is difficult to control?

....

b. Why is it difficult to control?

....

5. Who sets the policy and guidelines for email and web browsing at your workplace?

....

....

6. a. What is a computer virus?

....

....

b. What are three other names for them?

- ....
- ....
- ....

c. How can you protect your computer against them?

....

....

ISBN 9780170251594

5. Complete the crossword below.

Across

1 A system of interconnected computer networks

5 A computer software application (program) that allows users to view websites

6 A term that describes being connected to the Internet

7 The tool that allows users to exchange messages or computer files over a computer network

8 One of the four uses of the Internet

10 Unsolicited emails

11 Loading information from one computer onto another

13 The act of 'talking' over the Internet

Down

1 The Internet is a good source of this

2 Events that occur on the Internet at the same time as they occur in real life

3 A location on the Internet that allows users to access information

4 There are engines on the Internet that can do this for you

5 B2B refers to business to _____ e-commerce

9 The narrow strip across the top of a webpage that carries a logo, the website's name or advertising

12 An organisation that can provide you with e-commerce advice

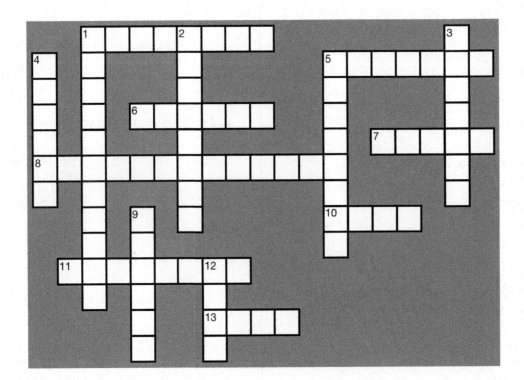

ISBN 9780170251594

8

Global links

8.1 The global consumer

1. Write down what is suggested by the cartoon above about Australia's place in the world.

....

....

2. Match the following words with their definitions.

exporting, global market, globalisation, importing, primary products, quotas, tariffs, trade

Limits placed on the amount of a product that can be imported.

....

The process of increased global interdependence between countries.

....

Selling domestically produced goods and services to overseas markets.

....

All natural resources, including the products of fishing, mining and agriculture.

....

The buying and selling of goods and services.

....

The buying and selling of goods and services on an international scale.

....

Buying goods and services from a seller overseas.

....

Taxes on imported goods meant to 'protect' locally produced goods against competition from overseas.

....

3. Name three areas in which there is evidence of globalisation.

- ....
- ....
- ....

4. Name three developments in shipping that have helped to increase world trade.

- ....
- ....
- ....

5. How have developments in communication promoted the growth of a global market?

....

....

6. Name three changes in government policy that have had a significant influence on world trade.

- ....
- ....
- ....

ISBN 9780170251594

7. a. Define the term 'transnational corporation (TNC)'.

....

....

b. Name four well-known TNCs.

....

....

....

....

8. a. Indicate whether the following terms are related to domestic or international trade.

exporting   ....

wholesaler   ....

retailer   ....

importing   ....

b. The diagram below shows the links between domestic and international trade but it has some important captions missing. Fill them in by using the following terms in the right place.

wholesaler   imports
customer   overseas markets

Domestic trade distribution

International trade distribution

9. Use the table below to answer the following questions.

a. List the items of export trade for Australia for 1986–87 from highest to lowest percentage.

....

b. Do the same for 2005–06.

....

c. In which area has there been the greatest percentage increase in exports from 1986 to 2006?

....

d. In which area has there been the greatest percentage decrease in exports from 1986 to 2006?

....

Year	Rural (%)	Resources/ Mining (%)	Manufact- uring (%)	Services (%)
1986–87	29.9	38.3	11.4	18.3
1992–93	20.8	32.1	16.1	21.2
1997–98	19.5	28.9	18.2	22.2
2000–01	18.6	32.5	17.9	21.4
2005–06	13.1	45.0	14.7	19.9

10.a. Why was Australia forced to seek new trade relationships in the 1960s?

....

b. Where, generally, did Australia find new trade relationships?

....

c. Eight of out ten of Australia's main trading partners are members of APEC. What is APEC?

....

ISBN 9780170251594

11. Insert each of the following labels in the appropriate place on the illustration below.

import sources, exports, export destinations, imports

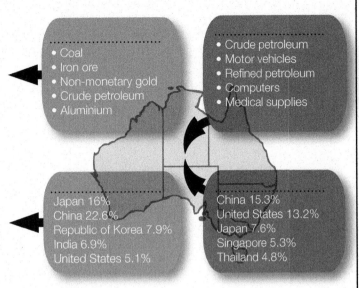

- Coal
- Iron ore
- Non-monetary gold
- Crude petroleum
- Aluminium

- Crude petroleum
- Motor vehicles
- Refined petroleum
- Computers
- Medical supplies

Japan 16%
China 22.6%
Republic of Korea 7.9%
India 6.9%
United States 5.1%

China 15.3%
United States 13.2%
Japan 7.6%
Singapore 5.3%
Thailand 4.8%

8.2 The global investor

1. Name two items, other than goods and services, that are sold on the global market.

- ....
- ....

2. Why are large sums of money transferred quickly from one country to another by traders?

....

....

3. What was the volume of foreign currency transactions in 2010?

....

4. a. Can a small investor invest money internationally?

....

b. Name three ways of doing this.

- ....
- ....
- ....

5. a. What is a limitation of investing only in the Australian share market?

....

....

b. What, by definition, are international shares?

....

c. With which countries are the following stockmarket names associated?

FTSE ....

All Ordinaries ....

Nikkei ....

Dow Jones ....

6. Refer to the table below.

Benefits of international shares	Risks of international shares
Can help to spread risk—overseas shares do not always rise and fall (fluctuate) at the same time as domestic shares. This can even out the gains and losses from share price fluctuations. Provides access to a wider range of industries than those listed on the Australian Securities Exchange. Offer higher average returns for long-term investments than domestic shares. Changes in **exchange rates** can result in large gains for investors when profits are converted back into Australian dollars.	Many of the world's stock exchanges don't trade in small volumes. Therefore, it may be difficult for traders to sell shares when they need to. International shares are more volatile than domestic shares; that is, their prices can rise and fall suddenly. Losses can be larger due to changes in the exchange rate. Remember, a loss of US$1000 on the New York Stock Exchange can be much larger when converted into Australian dollars. A devaluation of the Australian dollar would make these losses even larger.

a. What is one aspect of investing in international shares that can be either a benefit or a risk?

....

b. Why may it be difficult for traders to sell shares when they need to?

....

ISBN 9780170251594

c. Explain this statement: 'International shares are more volatile than domestic shares'.

....

7. a. Shares are examples of equity investments. What is meant by making an equity investment in a company?

....

....

b. What are four examples of interest-bearing investment?

- ....

- ....

- ....

- ....

c. What is their advantage over shares?

....

8. a. What type of investment is represented in the illustration on this page?

....

b. Name two advantages of investing in this way.

- ....

- ....

8.3 Transnational organisations

1. a. What is TNC the abbreviation for?

....

b. Explain what a TNC is.

....

....

c. List eight reasons why Australian businesses expand globally.

- ....

- ....

- ....

- ....

- ....

- ....

- ....

- ....

d. Name three differences between countries that make the management of global businesses a very complex task.

....

e. Name four other factors that have to be considered in successfully managing a global business.

....

2. a. Complete the following paragraph by adding the words below words in the correct places.

customising, balance, local, standardising

In the commercial environment, TNCs need to strike a

.... between .... their products and

marketing, and .... them to meet the needs

of the .... areas.

b. Explain how McDonald's has customised its menu for Norway.

....

3. A major financial issue for TNCs is the impact of fluctuations in the global business cycle. Name one advantage and one disadvantage of these fluctuations.

....

....

....

4. How are TNCs affected by legal issues?

....

....

5. Businesses are now expected to minimise their impact on the environment and adopt ecologically sustainable practices. Explain this term.

....

....

6. What are four advantages for TNCs in shifting their manufacturing overseas?

- ....
- ....
- ....
- ....

7. Write down what the illustration below tells you about 'sweatshop' working conditions.

....

....

....

ISBN 9780170251594

8. a. How much of a company's value, according to recent research, is related to its performance and assets?

....

b. Where is the remaining value?

....

....

....

c. How does transfer pricing help TNCs to minimise the tax they must pay?

....

....

d. What is the name given to countries where TNCs set up offices in order to take advantage of their low corporate tax rates?

....

9. a. Write down why the price of the imported goods has doubled in the above illustration.

....

....

b. Explain briefly how TNCs cope with this problem.

....

....

10. Name another problem TNCs might have to deal with. How do they cope with this problem?

a. ....

b. ....

....

8.4 International aid programs / 8.5 Current issues in globalisation

1. a. What is international or foreign aid?

....

....

....

b. Name the three main types of aid and briefly describe each one.

i. ....

....

ii. ....

....

iii. ....

....

c. What, then, do the letters NGO stand for?

....

....

d. Despite foreign aid having lots of benefits, there are some disadvantages. List four.

i. ....

....

ii. ....

....

iii. ....

....

iv. ....

....

2. a. Refer to the two diagrams below to answer the questions that follow.

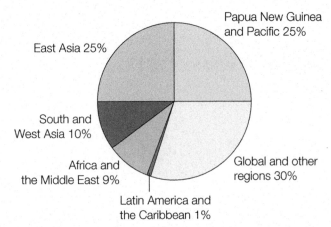

Where Australian aid was spent, 2010–2011

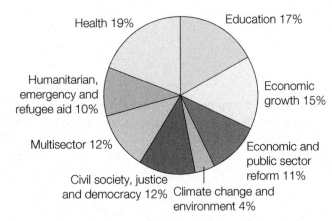

What Australian aid was spent on, 2010–2011

i. How much of Australia's aid goes to Papua New Guinea and the Pacific?

....

ii. What percentage of Australia's aid is spent on health and education?

....

ISBN 9780170251594

b. Refer to the diagram below to answer the questions that follow.

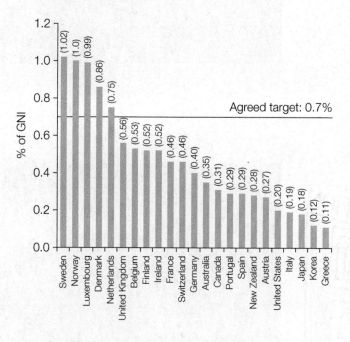

i. Which country gave the greatest percentage of its GNI as aid in 2011?

....

ii. Which country gave the lowest percentage of its GNP as aid in 2011?

....

iii. Which country gave approximately the same amount of aid as Australia in 2011?

....

3. a. There are three major criticisms of globalisation which focus on TNCs. What are three things that they are accused of?

i. ....

....

ii. ....

....

iii. ....

....

b. What are five arguments for globalisation?

i. ....

....

....

ii. ....

....

....

iii. ....

....

....

iv. ....

....

v. ....

....

....

ISBN 9780170251594

9

Towards independence

ACCOMMODATION

9.1 Moving from home /
9.2 Arranging accommodation

1. Fill in the bubbles in the illustration above with appropriate headings in relation to living independently.

2. The illustration above shows three unacceptable circumstances that may cause young people to leave home. What are four other reasons?

- ....
- ....
- ....
- ....

3. a. What is meant by 'guardianship'?

....

b. At what age do you become legally responsible for yourself, i.e. become an adult?

....

c. At what age can you legally leave home?

....

d. Under what two circumstances can you leave home if you are 16 years of age?

....

e. i. What is the name given to emergency accommodation run by community and church organisations?

....

ii. Who is eligible to use it?

....

4. a. Name two major factors in deciding where to live.

- ....
- ....

b. Name and describe three payments that are required before you rent a property.

- ....
- ....
- ....

c. What other costs could be involved?

....

ISBN 9780170251594

Fig. 1

Fig. 2

Paddington $300. Huge whole ground floor flat great character 4br + patio

Windsor 18-29yo. Male or Female, lge room in unit, built-in fan, very cls shop + trans, $100pw + exp, students ok

Bondi m/f 25 + shr 3brm hse $90pw

Castle Hill 1brm f/f own kit $150

Manly 1 br, Air cond granny flat, fully s.c. with fridge, quiet st cls to trains + shops. N/s, no pets or kids $165

Darlinghurst F 21-27 years F/T, n/s to shr 3 brm t'house with 2 others $85pw + $400 bond

Fig. 3

5. a. These three illustrations (above and left) show three ways of finding accommodation. What are they?

- ....
- ....
- ....

b. There is a fourth way too. What is it?

....

6. a. Define tenant.

....

b. Define landlord.

....

c. Define a residential tenancy agreement.

....

d. What two basic things do you agree to when you sign a residential tenancy agreement?

- ....
- ....

ISBN 9780170251594

e. How does a residential tenancy agreement protect the tenant?

- ....
- ....

f. What actions on a tenant's part can result in a tenant losing part, or all, of his/her bond?

- ....
- ....
- ....
- ....

g. Define blacklist.

....

6. a. What is 'task sharing' and why is it a good idea?

....
....
....

b. How successful do you think the share household in the illustration below would be?

....
....
....

9.3 Managing household finances

1. Match the following words with their definitions.

budget, economise, fixed expenses, insurance, lifestyle plan, variable expenses

- A contract that ensures payment in the event of some problem happening to you or your property.

....

- Cut back on spending to save money.

....

- A detailed plan of finances designed to ensure you don't spend more than you earn.

....

- A plan of commitments to help you manage your time without stress.

....

- Expenses that can vary.

....

- Expenses, such as rent, which can't vary.

....

2. a. Explain the difference between 'establishment costs' and 'ongoing expenses'.

Establishment costs:

....

Ongoing expenses:

....

b. Give three examples of ongoing expenses.

....

3. a. Give one strategy for managing ongoing expenses.

....

b. What is the aim of doing this?

....

c. Ongoing expenses can be subdivided into two categories. Name them. Give four examples of each.

.... expenses:

....

.... expenses:

....

4. Melissa wants to spend $250 per fortnight on food, $200 per month on clothes, $40 per month on a mobile phone and $50 per month on entertainment. She also wants to save $100 per month.

Melissa's yearly budget

Weekly income: $300.00

Fixed expenses	Total cost and payment interval	Cost per year
Rent	$400 per month	$____
Insurance on possessions	$100 per year	$____
Health insurance	$500 per year	$____
Transport	$450 per year	$____
Total yearly fixed expenses		$____
Variable expenses	**Total cost and payment interval**	**Cost per year**
Electricity	$20 per month	$____
Telephone	$50 per month	$____
Gas	$10 per month	$____
Food	$____ per fortnight	$____
Clothes and personal items	$____ per month	$____
Mobile phone	$____ per month	$____
Entertainment	$____ per month	$____
Savings	$____ per month	$____
Total yearly variable expenses		$____
Total yearly fixed expenses + total yearly variable expenses = $____		
Total yearly income – total yearly expenses = $____		

a. Is she earning enough money to do all this?

....

b. If your answer is 'Yes', how much can she save per year?

....

If your answer is 'No', by how much is she short per year?

....

c. If the answer to (a) was 'Yes', how much can she save per week?

....

If the answer to (a) was 'No', where can she cut down on expenses?

....

5. How can money be saved on

a. buying food ? List six ways.

- ....
- ....
- ....
- ....
- ....
- ....

b. entertainment? List two ways.

- ....
- ....

c. personal items? List four ways.

- ....
- ....
- ....
- ....

d. mobile phone? List three ways.

- ....
- ....
- ....

ISBN 9780170251594

6. Insurance is a way of making sure your income and property are protected. Name

   i. two types of insurance relevant to young people's health and state what they cover.

....

....

....

....

   ii. two types of insurance relevant to people's property.

....

....

....

....

©allesalltag/Alamy

b. What are two things to remember when making your decision on which brand or model to buy?

....

....

c. What can be an extra cost in major purchases that isn't part of the price?

....

9.4 Major purchases

1. It makes sense for people sharing a household to share the cost of providing furniture etc. but this can lead to problems. Describe how and when this can happen.

....

....

....

....

3. a. Name two ways of buying a major item if you don't have cash.

....

....

b. Explain the major difference between the two.

....

....

....

2. a. When is it a good time to purchase a new major item, such as a washing machine, so that you can buy it at the cheapest price?

....

....

....

....

c. Which of the two generally has a lower interest rate?

....

d. Explain the consequences of not paying on time regardless of how you buy a major item.

....

....

....

4. a. What is meant by a warranty?

....

b. What is the usual length of time for a warranty to last?

....

c. How can a warranty be extended?

....

d. Why should you always keep the receipt for any item purchased?

....

....

5. Explain why it is important to have insurance on items being paid for over a period of time.

....

....

....

....

....

Fig. 4 Second-hand may not be second best.

6. Explain the meaning of the caption on the above illustration. List the things you should you look out for when buying secondhand.

....

....

....

9.5 Community involvement and lifestyle issues

1. a. What do groups such as the St Vincent de Paul Society, The Smith Family, Rotary, the YMCA and the Department of Community Services have in common?

....

....

b. Name six other groups that offer the same type of services.

- ....

- ....

- ....

- ....

- ....

- ....

ISBN 9780170251594

2. Why do people become involved in voluntary organisations such as those listed in Question 1?

....

....

3. a. Why is time management very important when you are living independently?

....

....

b. In managing finances, it is sensible to create a budget. What is the name of a similar plan you can/ should create to manage your time?

....

c. As with a budget, your time is taken up with things you <u>must</u> do and things you <u>want</u> to do. List three items that belong on the 'must do' list.

- ....

- ....

- ....

Shutterstock.com/Julia Pivovarova

4. Name two things you would have to plan well before you could go on a skiing holiday.

....

....

5. Test yourself.

a. Match each of the following terms with the correct definition below.

bond	budget	classifieds
fixed expenses	landlord	lease
hire purchase	shelters	tenant
variable expenses	warranty	rent

- emergency accommodation run by community or church organisations

....

- advertisements in the newspaper arranged in columns under headings

....

- the document that outlines the terms under which you rent a property

....

- a person who rents a property

....

- a person who offers her or his property for rent

....

- the amount charged for accommodation in a house or apartment

....

- money you must pay up front when you move into a rental property

....

- a detailed plan of your finances listing all income and expenditure

....

- expenses that you cannot change

....

- expenses that you can change

....

- a guarantee to repair or replace a faulty item after purchase for a set period of time

....

- paying for a large item, such as a fridge, over a long period

....

b. Fill in the details missing from this chart.

```
┌─────────────────────────────────────┐
│ Reasons for leaving home            │
│   • ............................... │
│   • ............................... │
│   • ............................... │
└─────────────────────────────────────┘
                  ▼
┌─────────────────────────────────────┐
│ Questions to ask before leaving     │
│   • ............................... │
│   • ............................... │
│   • ............................... │
└─────────────────────────────────────┘
                  ▼
┌─────────────────────────────────────┐
│ Types of accommodation available    │
│   • ............................... │
│   • ............................... │
│   • ............................... │
└─────────────────────────────────────┘
                  ▼
┌─────────────────────────────────────┐
│ How to find accommodation           │
│   • ............................... │
│   • ............................... │
│   • ............................... │
└─────────────────────────────────────┘
                  ▼
┌─────────────────────────────────────┐
│ Before moving in                    │
│   • ............................... │
│   • ............................... │
│   • ............................... │
└─────────────────────────────────────┘
                  ▼
┌─────────────────────────────────────┐
│ After moving in                     │
│   • ............................... │
│   • ............................... │
│   • ............................... │
└─────────────────────────────────────┘
```

ISBN 9780170251594

10

Political involvement

10.1 The nature and structure of government in Australia

1. a. Define the term 'democracy'.

....

b. Where and when was the first democracy?

....

c. Explain, briefly, the difference between a direct democracy and a representative democracy.

....

....

d. Name the type of democracy we have in Australia.

....

e. Explain the essential foundations of democracy.

....

....

2. a. The place where the elected representatives meet is called:

....

b. The political leader of the federal government is called:

....

c. Describe how someone becomes Prime Minister.

....

....

d. Explain what the ministry is.

....

....

e. Explain what Cabinet is.

....

f. Name the other house of the federal government.

....

g. Name the city where the federal government meets.

....

3. a. The name given to the political leader of each state government is:

....

b. The name given to the political leader of each territory is:

....

c. As with the federal government, each state government, except one, has two Houses of Parliament. Which state does not?

....

4. a. The government of a local area (town or district) is called:

....

ISBN 9780170251594

b. The head of a council is called:

....

c. The head of a shire is called:

....

5. For each of the levels of government, list
a. the name of the leader.
b. the geographic area of responsibility of this level of government.
c. at least six responsibilities for this level of government.

Federal

a. ....

b. ....

c. ....

....

State

a. ....

b. ....

c. ....

....

Local

a. ....

b. ....

c. ....

....

10.2 Political action and decision making

1. a. Give three important rights we have because we live in a democracy.

  i. ....

  ii. ....

  iii. ....

b. State the general name for exercising these rights.

....

2. a. Define the term 'political party'.

....

....

ISBN 9780170251594

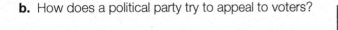

b. How does a political party try to appeal to voters?

....

c. Who, in general, do people vote for at election time?

....

3. State four ways in which an individual can influence decision making.

- ....
- ....
- ....
- ....

4. a. Define the term interest group.

....

....

b. Give three general examples of interest groups.

- ....
- ....
- ....

5. Name three ways in which the media plays a role in influencing government and decision making.

a. ....

....

b. ....

....

c. ....

....

6. a. Why is decision making a key factor in bringing about change? Give one reason.

....

....

....

b. The diagram below represents organisations which make or influence decisions that impact on the community. Write make(s) or influence(s) in the space in each box.

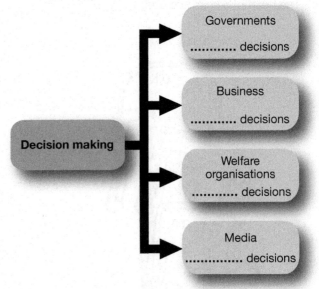

c. The diagram below shows the decision making process at state and federal levels of government. The following six words are missing.

Minister, policy, Inputs, Ministry/department, Cabinet, Parliament.

Insert the missing words into their correct places.

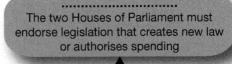

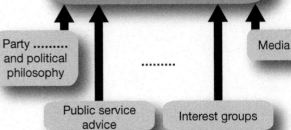

ISBN 9780170251594

10.3 Political parties

1. a. What is the chief means by which political power is exercised in Australia?

....

b. Create your own definition of the term 'political party'.

....

c. Name the four major political parties in Australia.

- ....
- ....
- ....
- ....

d. Which two work together as a coalition?

....

2. a. When was the Australian Labor Party (ALP) formed?

....

b. Why was it formed?

....

c. When was the first Labor Government elected?

....

d. Who was the first Labor prime minister?

....

e. Name six other Labor prime ministers.

....

....

3. a. When was the Liberal Party formed?

....

b. By whom?

....

c. Why?

....

d. When was the first Liberal government elected to power?

....

e. Who was the first Liberal prime minister?

....

f. Name two other famous Liberal prime minsters.

....

4. a. Give the year of the formation of the political party now known as the Nationals.

....

b. What was its name at that time?

....

c. What was the party's main aim?

....

d. Can the leader of the Nationals become prime minister?

....

e. What position can he/she hold if there is a Liberal/Nationals coalition elected?

....

5. a. When was the national organisation known as the Australian Greens formed?

....

b. When did Western Australia join this organisation?

....

6. Complete the following table.

Party Name	When formed	Who does the party generally represent?
Australian Labor Party		
Liberal Party		
Country/ National Party		
The Greens		

7. Explain how political parties help to make our political system more stable.

....

- ....
  ....
- ....
  ....

8. a. Define what an independent candidate is.

....
....

b. Why are these people, when elected, often referred to as crossbenchers?

....
....

10.4 Participation in the democratic process

1. a. At what age do Australians get the right to vote?

....

b. In which year did voting become compulsory?

....

2. a. What is a ballot paper?

....
....
....

b. What is **i.** an informal vote and **ii.** a donkey vote?

i. ....
....

ii. ....
....

3. a. What are the two main different ways of counting votes?

- ....
- ....

b. Which is the simpler or more straightforward of the two?

....

c. What change to voting was made in 1918?

....
....

80   Commerce.dot.com

ISBN 9780170251594

d. What is the basic difference between the two ways of counting votes when the voter is marking their ballot paper?

....

....

e. Which of the two methods requires a candidate to receive at least 50 per cent of the vote plus one vote?

....

4. a. What is the difference between preferential voting and optional preferential voting?

....

....

....

....

b. What method is used in NSW for the Legislative Council or Upper House?

....

c. Who determines the position on a ballot paper of a group or party?

....

d. There is a choice in completing a ballot paper with the optional preferential proportional representation.

i. Which method requires entering only one number on the ballot paper?

....

ii. Why would some people choose the other method?

....

HOUSE OF REPRESENTATIVES
Small green ballot paper

1	BROWN, JOHN
	NOVA, COSTA
2	NYAN, TAM
3	JONES, JENNY
	ESTERMANN, MIKHAIL

i

HOUSE OF REPRESENTATIVES
Small green ballot paper

	BROWN, JOHN
	NOVA, COSTA
	NYAN, TAM
x	JONES, JENNY
	ESTERMANN, MIKHAIL

ii

HOUSE OF REPRESENTATIVES
Small green ballot paper

1	BROWN, JOHN
4	NOVA, COSTA
2	NYAN, TAM
3	JONES, JENNY
5	ESTERMANN, MIKHAIL

iii

5. Three types of voting are represented by the ballot papers above. They are

- first-past-the-post

- preferential

- optional preferential voting

Correctly label each illustration.

i   represents   ....

ii   represents   ....

iii represents   ....

10.5 Interest groups

1. a. What percentage of Australians are members of a political party?

....

b. What is an alternative type of group that people can join?

....

c. What is the purpose of these groups?

....

....

....

d. Name one interest group that promotes the concerns of automobile owners?

....

2. Use the following words to complete the text below.

accountable, candidate, concerns, continuously, elections, influence, interest, issue, party, parties, political, views

.... groups are often compared with political .... because both are organisations that communicate the .... and .... of citizens to governments. But while political parties are .... to the electorate and seek to control the operations of government, interest groups lack this type of accountability. They are, instead, a .... force that seeks to .... government policies.

Interest groups have three features that set them apart from political parties:

- They don't seek to win ....

- They often campaign .... on issues, whereas political parties tend to be most active in the period immediately before elections.

- Interest groups are more .... orientated than political parties and depend on supporters who identify with their organisation. Political parties often depend on mobilising voters to support a particular .... or .... rather than any one issue.

3. Complete the table below to show **i.** the two main types of interest groups, **ii.** their general aims and **iii.** two general examples of area of concern of each.

i. Types	ii. Aims	iii. Examples

4. Match the following area of interest with some of their interest groups.

health (3), environment (2), education, children's welfare, media, firearms, Australian flag

Ausflag

....

Australian Child Protection Alliance

....

Australian Medical Association

....

Australian Nursing Federation

....

Diabetes Australia

....

Friends of the ABC

....

ISBN 9780170251594

Friends of the Earth

....

Gun Control Australia

....

National Tertiary Education Union

....

Wilderness Society

....

5. List ten ways in which interest groups can attempt to influence the decision-making processes of governments and large corporations.

a. ....

b. ....

c. ....

d. ....

e. ....

f. ....

g. ....

h. ....

i. ....

j. ....

6. Identify each of the following as an advantage **(A)** or disadvantage **(D)** of interest groups.

.... allows people to participate in decision-making processes

.... educates the public about certain issues

.... helps inform the government of the feelings of the electorate

.... keeps a check on government actions

.... may not be run democratically

.... may offer one-sided, or biased, information

.... may put their own interests before the interests of the majority of people

.... publicises ignored problems in society

.... represents minority groups who may not normally have much political influence

.... some groups have more power and influence than others

.... wealth, position and control of resources allow some groups to have a greater influence over government decision making

10.6 The media

1. a. The photo above shows examples of one main type of media. What is it?

....

b. What is the general name given to the other type of media which includes television and radio?

....

c. What is an important role of the media?

....

d. Describe, briefly, how the media and interest groups can help each other.

....

....

....

e. If the media highlights some issues and ignores others, they help shape the nature of public debate. What term is used to describe this role?

....

ISBN 9780170251594

2. a. Complete the following table to present an overview of the two main types of media, examples of each, their main area of focus and their use of images.

Type	Examples	Focus	Use of images

b. How can/do interest groups attract the attention of the media?

....

c. Which figure or illustration in your book shows this?

....

3. a. Use the following words to complete the passage below.

deregulation, economic, global, growth, media, merging, national, policy, regional, similarities, small, standardised, technological, transnational, vertical integration

It is mainly through the .... that viewers, listeners and readers have come to see themselves as a part of a .... and .... community.

Over the past 20 years, changing .... conditions and .... innovation have resulted in widespread change within the media industry.

The most significant change has been the shift in government media .... Under policies of ...., media companies have been encouraged to achieve .... by expanding the number of people they broadcast to, responding to consumer demand and maximising consumer choice. These policies have promoted the development of a new media order that is dominated by global interests rather than national and .... interests. An important feature of the new media is the dominance of a .... number of .... media enterprises competing on a global scale for power and profits.

These corporations concentrate on the .... between international markets that enable them to sell .... products across the globe.

Large media organisations are attempting to achieve global dominance by .... which involves one firm buying another to achieve control over the successive stages in the production of a good or service.

External diversification, on the other hand, involves the .... of information and entertainment industries with large telecommunications firms.

b. Name two concerns with this changing role of the media.

i. ....
....
....

ii. ....
....
....

ISBN 9780170251594

Travel

11.1 Travel destinations

1. Label the balloons in the illustration above with the issues that might concern a traveller.

2. a. Define

- tourism.

....

- domestic tourism.

....

- international tourism.

....

- ecotourism.

....

b. List six reasons why people want to travel.

- ....

- ....

- ....

- ....

- ....

- ....

3. a. Name five common sources of information for people who are trying to decide on travel destinations.

- ....

- ....

- ....

- ....

- ....

b. Which of the five sources you listed above would be most likely to give you brochures such as these?

....

c. Name one advantage and one disadvantage of using the Internet for travel information.

Advantage: ....

....

Disadvantage: ....

....

ISBN 9780170251594

d. Give one advantage that travel guides and family and friends have in common as sources of information.

....

....

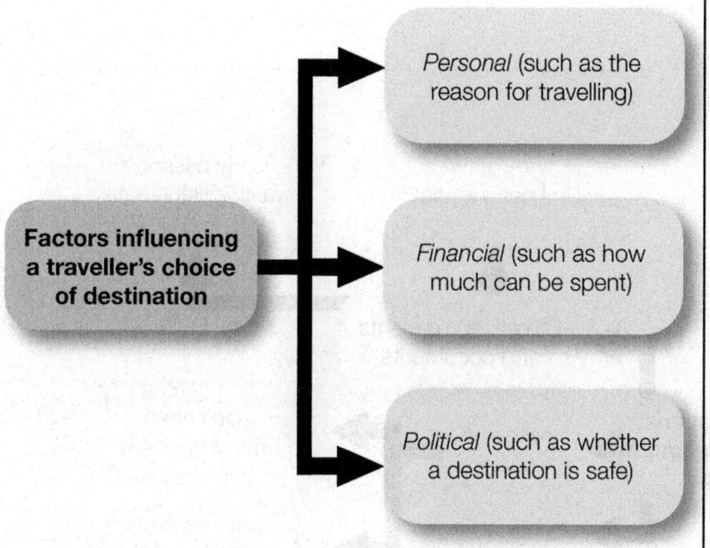

4. The diagram above represents three factors that influence a traveller's choice of destination.

a. Name three personal factors a traveller is likely to take into consideration when planning travel.

- ....

- ....

- ....

b. Which of the following is generally more expensive?

- domestic or overseas travel

....

- organised or self-planned tours

....

c. Concern for your personal safety is one political factor which could influence your choice of travel destination. Name one other political factor.

....

11.2 Planning a trip

1. 'Means of travel' covers both the method of transport and whether or not the traveller is part of a group or travelling independently.

a. Name one advantage and one disadvantage of each of these following methods of transport.

i. Air
- Advantage

....

- Disadvantage

....

ii. Ferry
- Advantage

....

- Disadvantage

....

b. i. What is another name for group travel?

....

ii. What is one advantage of group travel?

....

....

....

c. What is an itinerary?

....

d. What general name is given to people who prefer not to follow a predetermined itinerary when travelling?

....

....

ISBN 9780170251594

2. There are generally two choices in who actually organises a trip once the decision on destination has been made. You can organise it yourself or get a travel agent to do it. Name one advantage and one disadvantage of each.

a. Yourself
• Advantage

....

• Disadvantage

....

b. Travel agent
• Advantage

....

• Disadvantage

....

What type of insurance policy do I need?	Do I need travel insurance?
	Insurance
Is the destination safe?	
	Political stability
Is the culture significantly different from Australia's culture?	
	Culture

Considerations when planning a trip

Do I need a visa?	Is my passport valid until the date of my return?
Official requirements and documents	
Health and wellbeing	Do I need immunisations?
Language	Can I take my prescription medicines with me?
Will I be able to communicate?	Is the water safe to drink?

3. The diagram above illustrates things to consider when travelling.

a. Name two considerations regarding official documents.

....

....

b. Name three concerns relating to health and wellbeing

....

....

c. Name an important consideration relating to financial protection.

....

4. a. Explain the difference between a passport and a visa.

....

....

....

b. Name two different types of visa.

....

5. Name three ways you can protect yourself against health issues while you are travelling.

• ....

• ....

• ....

ISBN 9780170251594

6. Explain why understanding the culture of a country you are visiting is important.

....

....

7. Where is the best place to go to find out if there are any problems with travelling to some countries either for health or political reasons?

....

8. Name three major areas of expenses which are covered by travel insurance.

- ....

- ....

- ....

9. a. Indicate what the tourist depicted below should do before she takes the photograph.

....

....

b. Look at the illustration at top right and write down examples of the tourists' behaviour that the people in the temple would find offensive.

....

....

11.3 Organising an itinerary

1. Define the term itinerary.

....

....

2. a. Use the diagram on the next page to answer this question. List the five main areas of decision when planning an itinerary.

- ....

- ....

- ....

- ....

- ....

b. Name one important aspect of at least four of these decisions.

....

c. Name the system used to describe different levels of comfort in accommodation.

....

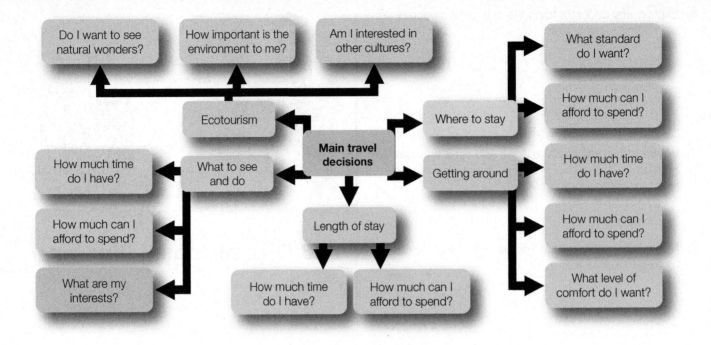

3. The following is an example of an itinerary for an overseas holiday.

FINAL ITINERARY FOR Mr and Mrs S Milton

Sat 09 Jun	10.05 pm	Depart Sydney on Trans-Pacific Airlines Flight TPA10
	9.55 pm	Arrive Los Angeles
09 –13 Jun		Midtown Thilon Hotel 400 South Hampshire Avenue
Wed 13 Jun	7.40 am	Depart Los Angeles on Trans-American Airlines Flight TAA24
	5.06 pm	Arrive Orlando International Airport
13 – 16 Jun		Maingate Lodge, West Charles Highway, Orlando
Sat 16 Jun	3.10 pm	Depart Orlando on Trans-Atlantic Airlines Flight TLA 819
	5.47 pm	Arrive New York (Newark)
	8.00 pm	Depart New York (Newark) on Trans-Atlantic Flight TLA 28
Sun 17 Jun	8.00 am	Arrive London Gatwick Airport
17Jun – 11 Jul		Radee House,153 Essex Gardens, London
Wed 11 Jul	10.00 pm	Depart London Heathrow on Trans-Asia Airlines Flight TFA 2
Thurs 12 Jul	6.15 pm	Arrive Singapore
	9.00 pm	Depart Singapore on Sing-Aus Airlines Flight SAA07
Friday 13 Jul	9.20 am	Arrive Sydney

ISBN 9780170251594

Answer the following questions based on the information in the itinerary on page 90.

a. When and where does this holiday begin and end?

....

b. It appears from the itinerary that the travellers will arrive in Los Angeles before they leave Sydney. Has the travel agent made a mistake or is there another explanation?

....

c. How long are the travellers staying in Los Angeles?

....

d. Where will the travellers stop next and at what time of day?

....

e. They then go on to London but have to transit (pass through) another airport first. Which one and where is it? When will they leave that airport?

....

f. Where do the travellers stay in London?

....

g. On their way home to Sydney, what happens in Singapore?

....

11.4 Solving travel problems

1. Name four major potential problems associated with travel.

- ....

- ....

- ....

- ....

2. a. What is the major problem created if you lose your passport?

....

b. Who should you contact first if any of your documents are lost or stolen?

....

c. Where do you go to obtain a new passport if yours is lost while you are travelling?

....

d. Where do you go if there is no Australian consulate or embassy in the country?

....

....

e. Who should you contact if you lose or have your tickets stolen?

....

f. What circumstances would make it necessary for you to contact your bank?

....

g. What are two steps you can take before leaving home to make replacement of documents easier?

....

....

ISBN 9780170251594

h. List three ways of avoiding theft.

* ....

* ....

* ....

3. a. Define the term exchange rate in relation to money.

....

b. Which currency is the Australian dollar most often related to in terms of its value?

....

c. What is a sensible thing to do before making any purchases overseas?

....

d. Name two ways, other than cash, of paying for purchases when travelling.

....

Robby Virus

4. a. Try to guess what the above sign indicates.

....

b. What is it important to remember about local laws when travelling?

....

c. If you get into legal trouble, who should be contacted?

....

d. An international driver's licence should be obtained before you leave Australia. Where do you go to get one?

....

5. How can you avoid problems which may arise when travelling in countries with very different cultural behaviours from those we are used to?

....

....

....

11.5 Current issues in tourism

1. Complete the following box by inserting the words below in the correct places.

> changing, culturally, destinations, dynamic, economic, ecotourism, exchange, health, issues, political, technological, terrorism

Tourism is very .... – it is constantly changing.

New .... are developed, while others become

less popular. Consumers' tastes are always

..............., as are our expectations of what we want

from the travel experience. These are some of the

current .... in tourism.

Such issues may revolve around changing tastes; for

example, the growth of .... and ....

sensitive tourism. .... issues include the impact

of .... rates and economic trends on the

number of people travelling. Issues related to

.... stability include the impact of ....

or war on people's travel plans. There are also

.... issues (such as outbreaks of disease in

certain destinations) and .... issues (such as

the development of larger planes or faster trains).

ISBN 9780170251594

2. a. Why does tourism, as an industry, rely very heavily on the environment?

....

b. What is meant by ecotourism?

....

....

c. Name another type of sustainable tourism.

....

....

d. Name two popular tourist places that are becoming examples of sustainable tourist destinations.

....

....

e. Explain one strict security measure at airports that was introduced after a 2006 terrorist threat.

....

....

Circle the correct answer for each multiple-choice question below.

3. What is an itinerary?

a. a list of activities available for tourists

b. a document allowing a person to travel overseas

c. issued by airlines detailing the cost of travel and the person's seat number on the flight

d. a plan for a person's trip, including destinations, travel arrangements and accommodation

4. What is the purpose of a travel agent?

a. act as a guide to people at tourist sites

b. help travellers plan their travel

c. assess the quality of accommodation and provide a star rating

d. provide legal assistance to travellers who get into trouble overseas

5. What is the exchange rate?

a. the amount charged by a travel agent

b. the rate of tax charged when departing a foreign country

c. the difference between the value of two currencies

d. the rating system used to indicate the quality of accommodation

6. Which of the following statements is true?

a. If you are arrested overseas the Australian Government will arrange your release.

b. If you are arrested overseas the Australian Government will pay all your legal expenses.

c. If you are arrested overseas the Australian Government will provide no assistance at all as travellers must obey local laws.

d. If you are arrested overseas the Australian Government will notify your family and provide contact details of local lawyers.

7. Which of the following best describes the purpose of a visa?

a. an approval to enter a foreign country

b. required before you can hire a car overseas

c. issued by the Australian Government to Australians to prove they are citizens

d. issued by travel agents on behalf of the Australian Government

Law in action

12.1 Contact with the law

1. a. Use the following words to fill in the gaps below.

18, actions, adult, critical, legal, legal capacity, majority, responsibilities, rights, vote

Once we reach the age of .... we are

considered old enough to have all the .... rights

of an adult. While age brings ...., it also brings

......................, including legal responsibilities. The

legal rights and responsibilities that come with the age

of a person are known as the person's ....

Eighteen is often seen as a .... age in Australia

because it is the age at which the law recognises

that a person is an .... This is known as

the age of .... At this age all the legal rights

associated with adulthood, such as the right to

..............., are granted. People aged 18 or older are

legally responsible for their ....

b. Determine which rights and responsibilities are being illustrated in the above cartoon.

....

....

....

2. a. In legal terms, why are the following ages significant?

10
....

14
....

16 •
....

•
....

•
....

17
....

18 •
....

•
....

•
....

b. Which age is known as the age of consent?

....

3. a. What crime is being committed in the illustration above?

....

b. If you are detained on suspicion of stealing, who is entitled to search you?

....

c. What is the maximum penalty for theft?

....

4. a. When a person is charged with a criminal offence, there is a burden of proof. What does this mean?

....

....

b. What two basics are necessary to prove guilt?

- ....

....

- ....

....

5. Insert the correct word from the following list into the six empty spaces on the figure below.

community service orders, bonds, periodic detention, fines, home detention, imprisonment

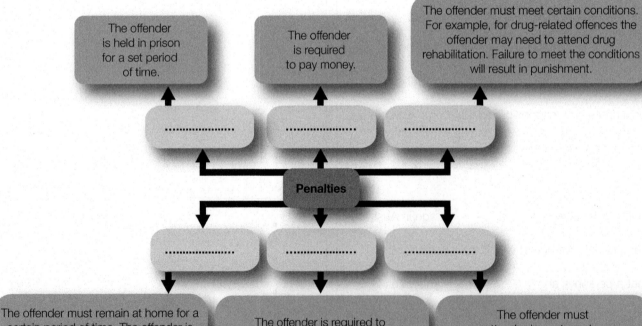

ISBN 9780170251594

6. Name three differences between civil law and criminal law.

- ....

- ....

- ....

7. a. What is the relationship between a contract and the law?

....

b. What do 'the offer', 'the acceptance' and 'the consideration' have in common in terms of a contract?

....

....

8. a. What is it called if our actions cause harm to other people or their property?

....

b. What are the two key factors required by law if someone wants to sue another for negligence?

- ....

- ....

12.2 Rights and responsibilities

1. a. Explain the difference between the rights of citizens in the USA and Australia.

....

....

b. What rights do Australian citizens have as consumers?

....

....

2. a. What is a basic responsibility in families of any type regarding the raising of children?

....

....

b. What basic right is every family member entitled to, but which up to 30 per cent of Australian families do not have?

....

....

c. What do the letters AVO stand for? Define AVO.

....

....

d. Name five responsibilities the law requires of parents for their children.

- ....

- ....

- ....

- ....

- ....

e. Under what circumstances can children be taken into care?

....

....

f. What rights do parents have so that they can effectively care for their children?

....

....

3. a. Which court deals with issues associated with the breakdown of marriages?

....

b. Define parenting orders.

....

....

4. List the four major rights and responsibilities of employees.

Rights

- ....

- ....

- ....

- ....

Responsibilities

- ....

- ....

- ....

- ....

5. a. Give another name for responsibilities that members of society should accept.

....

b. Name three areas of law setting out legal responsibilities of Australians.

....

c. Define statutory responsibility and give one example.

....

....

....

6. a. Whose responsibilities are more important in the legal system, those of the victim or those of the accused?

....

b. Define presumption of innocence.

....

....

....

c. Complete the following by listing the rights of the accused person and the victim.

Accused person
The right to:

- ....

- ....

- ....

- ....

Victim
The right to:

- ....

- ....

- ....

- ....

d. What is the main function of the law?

....

ISBN 9780170251594

c. Youth Justice Conferences

....

....

....

d. Mediation

....

....

....

e. Name the rights every person should be entitled to.

....

f. Whose role is it to promote these rights?

....

e. Conciliation

....

....

....

7. Name the first international document that specifically protected the rights of the child.

....

f. Tribunals

....

....

....

12.3 Resolving disputes

1. Write one or two sentences which summarise each of the following options for resolving disputes.

a. The police

....

....

....

b. The courts

....

....

ISBN 9780170251594

2. a. Mediation and conciliation have a number of similarities. Name five.

i. ....

ii. ....

iii. ....

iv. ....

v. ....

b. What modification of mediation and conciliation that has been introduced in New South Wales involves two mediators?

....

c. On what basis are these mediators selected?

....

12.4 Current issues relating to the law

1. Identify one major right that dying people do <u>not</u> have in Australia.

....

2. List three other legal issues that are commonly debated in our society.

....

....

....

....

....

ISBN 9780170251594

Our economy

13.1 The economic cycle

1. In one or two sentences, explain the sign in the above cartoon in your own words.

....

....

2. Insert the following words correctly into the blank spaces in the box below.

consumers, economics, exports, governments, imports, resources, satisfy, three

.... is a term that is generally used to refer

to how a nation tries to .... people's needs

and wants. There are .... main players in our

nation's economy – ...., businesses/employers

and .... – and they all work together trying to

solve the economic problem of choosing which needs

and wants to satisfy with their limited ....

A nation's economy is also affected by other nations'

economies through the trade of ....

and ....

3. a. List the four things that are generally regarded as economic resources.

....

b. Name three types of economy and identify which one of the three describes Australia's economy.

....

....

4. a. Name the three key players in our economy in the illustration below.

- ....

- ....

- ....

b. Name the two major activites related to our economy and the rest of the world.

- ....

- ....

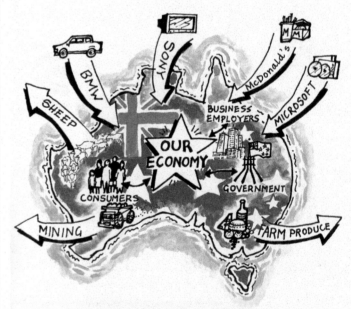

5. What is the relationship between supply and demand and the price of a product?

....

....

ISBN 9780170251594

Diagram 1

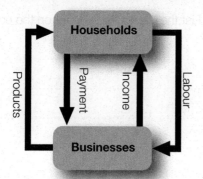

Diagram 2

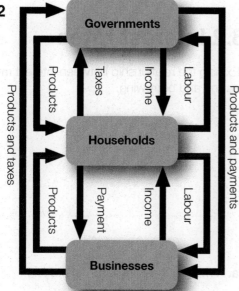

Diagram 3

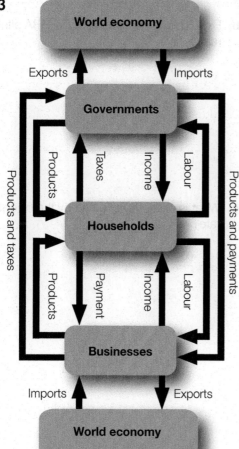

6. a. Which of the three diagrams illustrates Australia's link with the external economy? Which words in particular prompted your answer?

....

b. Which of the other two figures best represents Australia's internal economy? Why?

....

7. a. Name the two terms used to refer to the changes or fluctuations in economic activity that occur over time.

....

b. The four basic functions of an economy involve decision making. What are these four decisions?

....

....

c. What does the term total output refer to?

....

....

d. What is another term for total output?

....

e. GDP = C + I + G + (X – M). Change this equation into a sentence by replacing the letters with the words they represent.

....

....

....

f. What is it called when confidence in the economy is lacking for a sustained period and the GDP falls?

....

ISBN 9780170251594

g. Define inflation.

....

....

....

h. Why are wage rates now linked to productivity rather than to the price of goods and services?

....

....

i. Explain the link between unemployment and the economy.

....

....

8. a. Study the illustration below. Explain who is driving the Australian economy.

....

....

b. List the issues that impact on the economy.

....

....

....

....

....

13.2 Interest rates

1. Explain the relationship between interest rates and saving and borrowing.

....

....

....

....

2. a. What do the initials RBA stand for?

....

b. Explain how the actions of the RBA affect interest rates.

....

....

....

c. What is ultimately affected by the official interest rate?

....

....

ISBN 9780170251594

3. a. Briefly explain the difference between variable interest rates and fixed interest rates.

Variable interest rates

....

....

....

Fixed interest rates:

....

....

....

b. Which of the types of rates – variable and fixed - is generally higher and why?

....

....

....

c. Explain what is meant by honeymoon rate.

....

....

....

d. When is spending likely to increase – when interest rates are rising or falling and why?

....

....

....

e. Which investments become more popular when interest rates are low – term deposits, property or shares?

....

4. Match the phrases below into pairs, all of which refer to interest rates.

fixed rate, honeymoon rate, the higher the rate, variable rate

The longer the period

....

The lender can't change the rate

....

The lender can change the rate

....

Begins with low fixed rate then increases

....

13.3 Price changes

1. a. How is the real value of money defined?

....

....

b. When does the cost of living rise?

....

....

c. What do the letters CPI stand for? Explain briefly what the CPI is and what it measures.

....

....

....

d. The CPI was 100 in 1989–90. At the end of September 2010 it was 173.3. What does this mean?

....

....

e. What is a similar index used for measuring the changes in the cost of wages and salaries?

....

f. What does it indicate if the WPI is less than the CPI?

....

....

g. What is the aim of the RBA with regards to the level of inflation?

....

2. a. Define exchange rate.

....

....

b. If the Australian dollar increases in value what happens to the price of Australian imports?

....

c. What is the result of the Australian dollar depreciating?

....

....

....

3. Complete the following flow chart to show the implications of a fall in the value of the Australian dollar.

Value of Australian dollar falls

↓

consumers and businesses spend ....
on ....

↓

.... in spending on local products

↓

consumption and .... rise;

Australian products become relatively ....
to foreign buyers

↓

.... in exports

↓

.... economic activity in Australia;
increased demand for .... products

↓

pressure on .... due to the problem of
allocating scarce resources

↓

adjustment of ....

↓

possible excessive ....

ISBN 9780170251594

13.4 Current issues relating to changes in economic activity

1. Fill in the spaces in the text below with the listed words.

community, developing, economic, environmental, implications, political, pollution, prices, social, unemployment

Many economic issues have .... beyond what is traditionally thought of as 'economics'. .... and .... aspects of economic issues, for example, are often not addressed or taken into account by economists. For example, the impact of .... on family and .... relationships are rarely considered in economists' discussions of the labour market.

.... factors are also not fully taken into account in most economic models and data. Damage to our environment is not generally considered when .... of products are determined, and impacts on the environment from damage caused by .... are not usually included in .... data. 'Environmental economics' is slowly .... as economists tackle these environmental issues.

2. a. Explain the message in the illustration above regarding the economy and the environment.

....

....

....

b. List four effects on the environment from the factory in the illustration. It has:

- ....
- ....
- ....
- ....

3. Use the clues to complete the crossword.

Across

2 A fall in the value of money because general prices have risen

5 The main measure of inflation in Australia

8 Interest _____

9 Entrepreneurial skill

12 The term used to describe the tendency of economies to move through periods of boom and slump over a period of time (two words)

13 A measure of economic activity within Australia; also known as total output

15 A _____ of a currency is when one currency's value falls in terms of another currency

17 The number of workers without a job who are willing and able to work

Down

1 An _____ of a currency is when one currency's value rises in terms of another currency

3 Businesses undertake this when they purchase capital equipment, such as factories

4 The price of one currency in terms of another currency (two words)

6 A _____ economy is a system where resources are owned by households

7 An economy where resources are owned by both private individuals and the government

10 The pay you receive per time period of work (two words)

11 One of the factors of production. It includes machines, factories and offices

14 Two consecutive quarters of negative economic growth

16 Goods, services and capital assets purchased from overseas

18 Goods, services and capital assets sold overseas

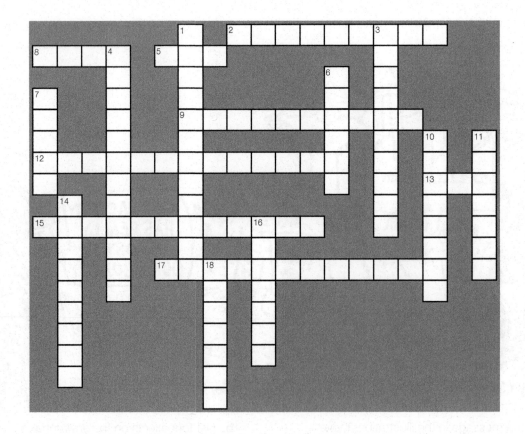

ISBN 9780170251594

Community participation

14.1 Non-profit organisations

1. The above illustration shows two of the many non-profit organisations that help people. Name these organisations and a service that each offers.

....

....

....

2. a. Define the term 'non-profit organisation'.

....

....

....

b. Which two of the following adjectives <u>cannot</u> be accurately used to describe non-profit organisations?

not-for-profit, political, autonomous, self-governing, non-political, government-controlled

....

c. Match the following non-profit organisations with their area of activity.

The Smith Family, ActionAid, Landcare Australia, Country Women's Association, Friends of the ABC

• meeting local, community-based needs

....

• meeting the welfare needs of the disadvantaged

....

• caring for the environment

....

• meeting the needs of the oppressed and disadvantaged on a global scale

....

• cultural advancement/promotion

....

d. What general role within society do non-profit organisations fulfil?

....

3. Non-profit organisations can be categorised according to the scale at which they operate – local, national or international. At which level do the following operate?

RSPCA ....

RSL ....

Greenpeace ....

Rotary ....

4. a. What four factors do non-profit organisations need in order to be successful?

i. ....

ii. ....

iii. ....

iv. ....

b. What other factors are needed for non-profit organisations to reach their potential?

....

....

ISBN 9780170251594

5. One international non-profit organisation is the Red Cross.

a. Where does it get its funding?

....

b. When was the Red Cross founded ?

....

c. Who recommended its establishment and why?

....

....

....

....

d. What is the symbol for the Red Cross and what does it represent?

....

....

....

e. How many members and volunteers are there in the Red Cross internationally?

....

f. What are the four main areas in which the Red Cross is involved?

   i. ....

   ii. ....

   iii. ....

   iv. ....

14.2 Active community participation

1. a. A community is made up of people who share something in common. What name is given to a community who live in the same neighbourhood?

....

b. What is the other type of community?

....

....

c. Can someone be part of both types of community? Explain your answer.

....

....

....

d. What important feeling do people get from being part of a community?

....

2. One type of community group is one which is concerned about an issue and wants change. Why is a community group more likely to have success than an individual in raising concern and getting changes made? Give two reasons.

a. ....

....

....

b. ....

....

....

ISBN 9780170251594

3. With the world becoming increasingly interconnected, we are now part of a global community. What are the essentials of being a good or informed global citizen?

....

....

....

4. a. What are the benefits of working together with other people, whether in an organisation, a class, a hobby group etc? Fill in the gaps below.

- You get a sense of ....:

- You meet people with similar ....:

- You achieve .... that you couldn't attain by yourself.

- You know that you have helped make

  a ....:

- You develop skills that can be .... to other aspects of life.

- You develop an understanding of

  .... processes.

b. What will be the outcome if you have a complete understanding of both the aims of an organisation of which you are a member and your role within the organisation?

....

c. Your textbook outlines eight key stages that need to be worked through for an organisation to achieve a successful outcome. Eight key words or phrases relating to these key stages are listed below. Rearrange them into their correct order.

analyse and present, deadlines, decide, evaluate, implement, information, strategies, time frame

....

....

d. Briefly explain what each person in the above illustration is responsible for.

Task co-ordinator:

....

....

Team member:

....

....

Networker:

....

....

Evaluator:

....

....

ISBN 9780170251594

14.3 Goal setting

1. a. Give four reasons why goal setting is important.

....
....
....
....

b. Explain the difference between long-term goals and short-term goals.

....
....
....
....

c. Name the series of steps which outline what is necessary for an organisation to achieve its objectives.

....

d. List four strategies for achieving objectives.

....
....

e. Read through the nine qualities of an effective leader listed on page 291 of your textbook. Summarise these qualities below. The first one is done for you.

- communicate
- ....
- ....
- ....
- ....
- ....
- ....
- ....
- ....

2. a. Give a reason why organisations hold meetings.

....
....

b. Define 'AGM' and explain what happens at this event.

....
....

c. The following terms relate to the meetings of an organisation. Define them.

Agenda:

....

....

Constitution:

....

....

Standing orders:

....

....

Quorum:

....

....

Minutes:

....

....

Meeting procedures:

....

....

Motion:

....

....

Amendment:

....

....

3. a. What is the advantage of negotiation as a strategy for achieving objectives?

....

....

b. What is the one single most important necessity in order to achieve a successful negotiation?

....

c. In planning a negotiation, there are a number of steps to consider.

   i. Two of them involve compromise. What are they?

....

....

   ii. Two of them involve preparing arguments. What are they and why are there two?

....

....

4. a. Which other strategy for achieving objectives needs a similar set of steps to those for negotiation to be followed?

....

ISBN 9780170251594

b. What is the basic difference between this and negotiation?

....

....

5. In what two ways can citizens use the political process to achieve these objectives?

- ....

....

- ....

....

6. What is the aim of the speaker's talk in the situation above?

....

....

14.4 Achieving community outcomes

1. Non-profit community-based organisations have different ways of achieving their different aims. How do the following groups achieve their aims?

a. Trade unions:

....

b. Charities:

....

c. Service clubs:

....

2. How can individuals become involved in non-profit community-based organisations? Name three ways.

- ....

- ....

- ....

3. The majority of non-profit community-based organisations were formed to meet a particular community need. Why were the following organisations formed?

a. The NSW Rural Fire Service:

....

....

b. World Vision:

....

....

4. a. What is one of the best-known fundraising events for World Vision?

....

ISBN 9780170251594

b. List six other ways in which community members can assist World Vision.

....

....

....

....

....

....

5. Select the correct word from the list below to match each of the definitions in the next column. This will create a glossary of terms relating to organisations.

goal	negotiation	president
action plan	community	treasurer
campaign	resolution	lobbying

.... an outline of short-term and long-term goals

.... an organised course of action for a specific purpose

.... a group of people who share something in common

.... the outcome an organisation or individual wishes to achieve

.... the activity individuals and organisations engage in to influence decision makers

.... a series of communications that produce an agreement that all parties consider acceptable

.... the elected head of an organisation

.... a motion that has been supported by a meeting

.... the office bearer responsible for the finances of an organisation

6. Imagine there has been a proposal to set up a late night computer game parlour in your local shopping centre. Fill in each speech bubble to express the points of view of some people in the community.

ISBN 9780170251594

Running a business

15.1 Being an entrepreneur

1. List two things that the above illustration tells you about Zoe's business. What information does it give about the success of her business?

....

....

2. a. Define the term 'entrepreneur'.

....

....

   b. What makes entrepreneurs different from other people?

....

   c. What do they do?

....

....

....

3. a. Use the words from the list below to fill in the spaces in the text below.

also, bosses, control, goals, hours, independence, lose, money, risk, regulations, satisfaction, stress, uncertainty, work

.... is one of the key reasons people go into

business for themselves. Entrepreneurial talents,

skills, ideas and energies are directed towards the

entrepreneurs' own .... Entrepreneurs can

find great personal .... in seeing their ideas

come to fruition, under their own ....

Being self-employed gives people the chance to

make much more .... than they could as

someone else's employee. However, it also carries a

financial .... If the business is unsuccessful,

the entrepreneur will .... the funds invested in

the business. If money has been borrowed from family

and friends, their funds could .... be lost.

Running a business often means long ....,

hard ...., ... and .... Even

though self-employed people are their own

..................., they have to deal with the demands of

customers, suppliers, ... and financiers.

   b. What is a financier?

....

....

ISBN 9780170251594

4. a. List nine adjectives that describe some of the characteristics often possessed by an entrepreneur.

....

....

....

b. Choose adjectives from your answer to 4. a. that you think could be applied to Lisa in the above illustration. Give reasons. List any other adjectives you would use to describe her and her enterprise.

....

....

....

....

....

....

15.2 Planning for success

1. a. Explain the challenge in identifying a new business opportunity.

....

....

....

....

b. To identify a business opportunity, there are five factors to consider as shown in the diagram below.

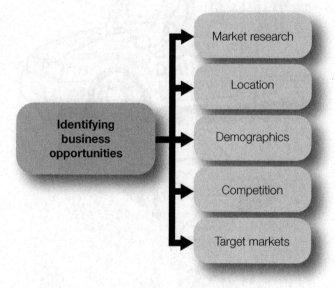

Write one sentence explaining each factor in your own words.

Market research:

....

Location:

....

Demographics:

....

....

Competition:

....

....

Target markets:

....

2. a. What options, in terms of structure, are available for someone setting up a new business?

....

b. Which type of structure has Joe in the above illustration chosen for his business? How can you tell?

....

c. What are some other examples of similar businesses?

....

....

3. Architects, accountants, lawyers and doctors often select a structure where two or more people contribute to the running of the business. What is this structure called?

....

4. a. By which abbreviated phrase can you identify the business structure known as a private company?

....

b. What is the phrase in full? What does it mean in practical terms?

....

....

5. What is a basic difference between a private and a public company?

....

....

....

....

6. What type of business structure would suit a sporting or gardening club that wished to trade? Why?

....

....

....

....

7. Which business structure is the least costly to set up?

....

ISBN 9780170251594

8. If you decide to buy a business that is already set up, you pay for 'goodwill'. What does this mean?

....

....

9. a. One type of business that can be purchased is a franchise. What does this mean?

....

....

b. Gives reasons why a franchise might not be a good business enterprise for an entrepreneur.

....

....

10. Before commencing operations, what two major needs have to be met?

....

....

15.3 Business operation

1. In Australia, the operations of businesses are regulated by all three levels of government – federal, state and local.

Indicate which of the three levels of government are related to the following business areas by writing federal, state or local in the spaces provided.

town planning

workers compensation   ....

Australian business number   ....

superannuation   ....

workplace health and safety ....

fire regulations   ....

income tax   ....

parking   ....

GST   ....

business name   ....

2. a. Having set up a business, the product then needs to be marketed. What are the four Ps of marketing?

- ....

- ....

- ....

- ....

b. With which of these four Ps are the following words associated?

i. packaging   ....

ii. deliveries   ....

iii. advertising   ....

iv. public relations ....

v. appearance   ....

vi. competitive   ....

vii. easy access   ....

viii. 'freebies'   ....

3. a. The following are just some of the records which businesses have to keep.

Write a brief definition of each.

i. profit and loss statement:

....

....

....

ii. balance sheet:

....

....

iii. cash flow statement:

....

....

ISBN 9780170251594

b. With which of the business records identified on page 121 are the following equations associated?

    i. revenue − expenses = profit or loss

....

    ii. assets = liabilities + capital

....

c. Define the terms revenue, assets, liabilities and capital.

revenue:

....

assets:

....

liabilities:

....

capital:

....

4. a. What are some events that can cause disruption to a business?

....

b. Define risk management.

....

....

c. What is one of the most common ways for businesses to protect themselves against loss caused by disruption to business?

....

5. Outline three results of good record keeping.

- ....
- ....
- ....

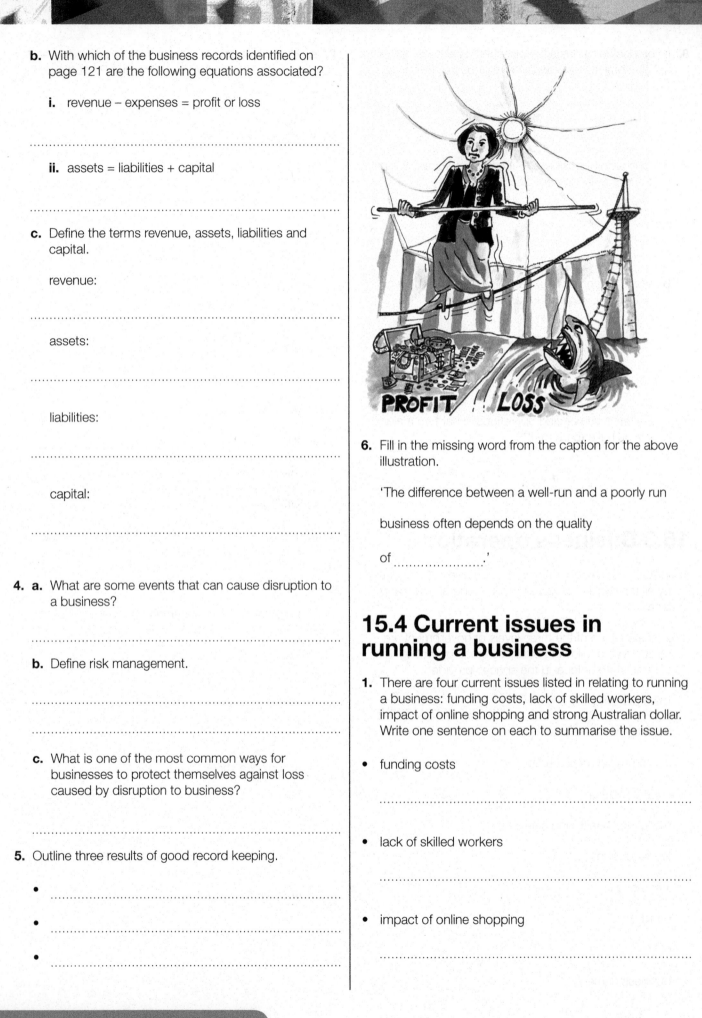

6. Fill in the missing word from the caption for the above illustration.

'The difference between a well-run and a poorly run

business often depends on the quality

of ....'

15.4 Current issues in running a business

1. There are four current issues listed in relating to running a business: funding costs, lack of skilled workers, impact of online shopping and strong Australian dollar. Write one sentence on each to summarise the issue.

- funding costs

....

- lack of skilled workers

....

- impact of online shopping

....

ISBN 9780170251594

- strong Australian dollar

....

2. a. Which two industries are most affected by the impact of the high Australian dollar?

....

   b. What are businesses doing to overcome the problems brought about by the high Australian dollar?

....

Use the clues to complete the crossword.

Across

1 The term used to describe individual owners of a private or public company

6 The name given to a business owned and operated by two or more people

9 A company listed on the stock exchange (two words)

10 The collective name given to anything owned by a business, including its equipment, stock and bank deposits

12 The situation where a business is no longer able to pay its creditors

15 One of the four Ps of marketing

16 The analysis of a business's potential strengths, weaknesses, opportunities and threats (initials)

17 A business that exists separately from its owners

Down

2 The process involved in identifying, controlling and minimising the impact of uncertain events (two words)

3 The study of a population and its characteristics

4 A person who organises and manages an enterprise

5 A statement listing all the assets, liabilities and capital of a business (two words)

7 The amount that a business owes to lenders and suppliers

8 The term used to describe someone who owns and runs their own business (two words)

11 Suppliers of goods and services to a business

13 The movement of cash into and out of a business (two words)

14 The money or other assets used to fund the establishment or expansion of a business

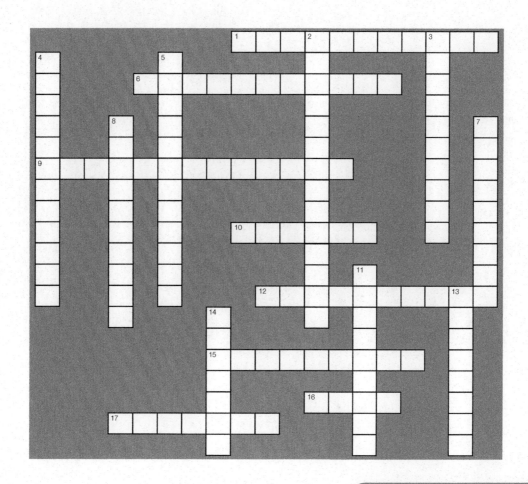

ISBN 9780170251594